ENDING OBAMA'S WAR

ENDING OBAMA'S WAR

RESPONSIBLE MILITARY WITHDRAWAL FROM AFGHANISTAN

David Cortright

Paradigm Publishers

Boulder • London

Copyright © 2011 Paradigm Publishers

Published in the United States by Paradigm Publishers, 2845 Wilderness Place, Boulder, CO 80301 USA.

Paradigm Publishers is the trade name of Birkenkamp & Company, LLC, Dean Birkenkamp, President and Publisher.

Library of Congress Cataloging-in-Publication Data

Cortright, David, 1946–
  Ending Obama's war : responsible military withdrawal from Afghanistan / David Cortright.
    p. cm.
  Includes bibliographical references and index.
  ISBN 978-1-59451-984-0 (hardcover : alk. paper)
  1. Afghan War, 2001—Peace. 2. United States—Military policy. 3. Disengagement (Military science) 4. Postwar reconstruction—Afghanistan. 5. Afghanistan—Social conditions—21st century. 6. Women—Afghanistan—Social conditions—21st century. 7. National security—Afghanistan. I. Title.

  DS371.412.C66 2011
  958.104'7—dc22

                                                          2011008022

Printed and bound in the United States of America on acid-free paper that meets the standards of the American National Standard for Permanence of Paper for Printed Library Materials.

Designed and Typeset by Straight Creek Bookmakers.

15 14 13 12 11   1 2 3 4 5

Contents

Preface

This book is the result of my personal journey to understand the complexities of the war in Afghanistan and how to bring it to an end in a responsible manner. It began as an attempt to evaluate the ethics of the war and evolved into a broader attempt to articulate an alternative course. For years I had remained silent about Afghanistan, focusing as many of us did on the war in Iraq. The Bush administration's invasion and occupation of Iraq were so obviously unjust that we had to speak out. The military campaign in Afghanistan seemed more ambiguous and therefore less objectionable. It was justified as a necessary fight to suppress al Qaeda and help the Afghan people, especially women, create a future free of Taliban extremism. The closer I looked at the Afghanistan War, however, and as President Obama sharply escalated U.S. military involvement, the more I began to question these assumptions. As my doubts and concerns multiplied, I embarked on an intensive study that led me to the observations and conclusions contained in this volume. Along with many others I recognized the need for an alternative policy, one that could end the war without making matters worse and help achieve a more just and secure future for the people of the region.

While this is my personal exploration, and I take full responsibility for any errors of fact or judgment that may be contained here, the book is very much a collective effort that has involved dozens of colleagues, friends, and associates. I am grateful to the Peace Research Institute of

Oslo (PRIO) and the Aquinas Center at Ave Maria University in Naples, Florida, for inviting me to speak at the June 2009 conference "Just War in the Catholic Tradition," and especially to Greg Reichberg, the principal organizer of the conference, for graciously accepting my request to write a paper applying just war ethical principles to the Afghanistan war. I also thank Henrik Syse at PRIO and Martin Cook, former professor of military ethics at the U.S. Air Force Academy, for reviewing an early version of the ethics portion of the manuscript.

I benefitted most in writing this book from my colleagues at the Kroc Institute for International Peace Studies at Notre Dame, especially Sarah Smiles Persinger and Eliot Fackler. Smiles Persinger helped to write Chapter Three and has been an invaluable ally in researching and writing about the gendered dimensions of the war. A former journalist for the *Melbourne Age* with several years of experience reporting in the Middle East, Smiles Persinger traveled to Kabul in April and May 2010 to research security and women's rights issues. A specialist in war and gender issues, she conducted more than fifty interviews with Afghan women leaders, including parliamentarians, activists, school principals, health workers, and members of the police force and army. Eliot Fackler is research assistant to the policy studies program at the Kroc Institute and has been an invaluable colleague in this and other research and writing projects at the Institute. He edited and researched every page and reference in this book and played an indispensable role in managing the production of the manuscript. This work would not have been possible without his enthusiastic professional support and assiduous attention to detail.

Support for this project also came from Hal Culbertson, executive director of the Kroc Institute, and Joan Fallon, the Institute's director of communications. Assisting with research were current and recent Kroc Institute MA students Takhmina Shokirova, Vanya Cucumanova, Lucia Tiscornia, and Shashi Rani Regmi. Colleagues at the University of Notre Dame who shared perspectives and insights include Dan Lindley, Mary Ellen O'Connell, Peter Wallensteen, and Michael Desch. Duane Shank, senior policy advisor at Sojourners, read an early version of the manuscript and provided helpful comments and critiques. Also providing constructive suggestions and critiques was Bob Haywood, executive director of the One Earth Future Foundation. I received valuable insights and assistance from Alistair Millar and Linda Gerber-Stellingwerf of the Fourth Freedom Forum, and from Tom Andrews of the Win Without War coalition. I benefitted from an important briefing session and discussion at the Center for International Policy with Matt Hoh, Matt Waldman, Selig Harrison, Bill Goodfellow, and Gary Porter. Celeste Kennel Shank provided editing assistance.

Financial support for the research and writing of this manuscript came primarily from the Kroc Institute. I am deeply grateful to the Institute's director, Scott Appleby, for his support and encouragement of my work. The Dutch development agency Cordaid also provided assistance. We are very grateful for the support and encouragement of the Cordaid staff team, including Lia van Broekhoven, Paul van den Berg, Dewi Suralaga, and Fulco van Deventer.

Introduction

I have spent most of my life working against war, from Vietnam to Iraq, but I am deeply torn about what should be done in Afghanistan. I recoil at the specter of a seemingly endless war, now in its tenth year, increasingly violent and destructive, with casualties rising and extremism spreading in the region and beyond. Yet military withdrawal could make matters worse if it leads to the return of the Taliban, handing victory to those who harbored al Qaeda on 9/11, and abandoning Afghan women to the tyranny of misogynist reactionaries. Is war the right strategy, though? We have battled the Taliban for more than nine years, yet they only seem to grow stronger and widen their influence. How can we succeed when our supposed allies in Kabul are unreliable and corrupt and in some cases espouse policies that differ little from those of the Taliban? Is this a struggle worthy of the sacrifices of our soldiers and the vast effort being poured in by dozens of countries?

The initial military action after 9/11 seemed like a justifiable response to the killing of nearly 3,000 Americans. It was an act of self-defense and an attempt to prevent future attacks. At the time I urged greater reliance on international law rather than unilateral force, but I did not protest when bombing strikes began a few weeks later. Like most people I was glad to see the end of the Taliban regime and welcomed what seemed like the beginnings of a more reasonable government in Kabul.

Then came Iraq. As the Bush administration prepared its ill-fated war of choice, most of us turned toward trying to prevent the looming disaster. I helped create the Win Without War coalition to lobby against the invasion and coauthored reports showing that sanctions and inspections were effective means of constraining Iraq's weapons programs. All to no avail as the unlistening Bush administration plowed ahead with its preplanned invasion and occupation.

For several years we remained fixated on Iraq, organizing protests and vigils against the occupation, reacting with horror as insurgency and civil war engulfed the country. We worked politically to elect progressive candidates in 2006, which tipped control of the U.S. Congress to the Democratic Party. We provided the core constituency for Barack Obama, who built his campaign and won early primaries partly on the basis of his pledge to end the war in Iraq.

Meanwhile, Afghanistan descended into chaos. A limited military mission to drive out al Qaeda and the Taliban morphed into a prolonged occupation, but with U.S. forces starved of resources to feed the folly of Iraq. As insurgency began to spread—backed by the Pakistani military and intelligence services—violence and destruction increased. The terror of Iraq—suicide bombings, improvised explosive devices (IEDs), and car bombings—began to appear in Afghanistan, as if some lethal virus of violence had leaped across borders. The war in Iraq was slowly coming to an end, but armed conflict in Afghanistan was spiraling out of control.

I began to have doubts about the efficacy and morality of this enlarged military mission. Responding to attacks by al Qaeda was one thing, but an open-ended war against a Taliban-led insurgency was quite another. The greater the number of troops deployed, the worse the security situation seemed to become. Could the initial self-defense justification of October 2001 be extended to the current large-scale counterinsurgency campaign? What political good would be gained by continuing and escalating military violence? When an invitation came last year to speak at a conference on just war doctrine I leaped at the opportunity to conduct an ethical evaluation of the war. The resulting analysis deepened my skepticism and intensified my quest for alternatives.

When we discuss possible military withdrawal, the conversation inevitably turns to the fate of Afghan women. The U.S.-led intervention ended the barbaric policies of the Taliban and created new opportunities for Afghan women. Without security protection, women in Afghanistan could be returned to the dark ages and subjected to grotesque cruelties. Public stoning, marauding gangs of Taliban thugs, prohibitions against schooling and employment—all would return, many fear, if the United States and its allies leave. Military exit will not bring peace if it means abandoning Afghan women.

One of my purposes in writing this volume is to build unity and shared understanding among peace advocates and defenders of women's rights. For decades antiwar and human rights activists have stood together in opposition to militarism and oppression, but in recent years we have found ourselves if not on opposite sides at least with some differences about whether to support the U.S. military presence in Afghanistan. In 2009 we had a discussion within the Win Without War coalition in which I found myself debating the Obama troop surge with colleagues from Feminist Majority, a group I have long admired. In the end the coalition agreed on a unified call for reducing the U.S. military footprint in Afghanistan and increasing support for diplomacy, development, and human rights, but the experience was disorienting. Because peace and human rights are inseparable, our movements must work together. Peace advocates must recognize the necessity of defending the rights of Afghan women, and human rights defenders must acknowledge the need to demilitarize U.S. strategy. Combining these approaches offers the best hope for enhancing both justice and security.

But how can we protect Afghan women and oppressed minorities in Afghanistan if we withdraw militarily? It seems like an insoluble dilemma. Most of us are not absolute pacifists. Occasions arise when the use of force—targeted and proportional—may be justified, for self-defense of course, but also to protect civilians and to end or prevent mass killing. In many parts of the world resistance to invasion and occupation is considered a just cause. Sometimes military force is necessary to achieve a higher good. Is this the case today in Afghanistan? It may have been true in October 2001, but is it still true ten years later?

This volume is an attempt to resolve these moral and political dilemmas. I use the framework of just war doctrine to evaluate the current military mission and explore alternatives. I summarize the broad consensus that exists among military and policy experts that the war is unwinnable and is exacerbating the very dangers we hope to diminish. That part of the argument is increasingly evident, which explains why growing numbers of people in the United States and around the world are turning against the war. The bigger question is whether viable alternatives exist that can enhance security in the region and preserve the fragile gains of Afghan women. I believe such alternatives are available, and I devote much of the volume to explaining what they are. A range of options exist—diplomatic, political, economic, and social—that can help to achieve greater security and stability in Afghanistan while protecting human rights. I examine these options as a way of clarifying my own thinking but also in the hope that they can point toward a better way forward.

Obama's War

As this manuscript was being written, a grim milestone was reached. U.S. casualties in Afghanistan during the Obama administration surpassed those of the Bush era. During the eight years of the Bush administration, total U.S. fatalities in Afghanistan numbered 617. By mid-September 2010, fatalities during the Obama administration surpassed 620, and they have continued to rise. Barack Obama did not start this war, but he embraced it as a just cause on the campaign trail in 2008 and sharply escalated U.S. involvement soon after taking office. This is his war, and its ultimate fate will significantly shape his presidency and place in history.

The irony is that the president himself is skeptical of military solutions. During his fall 2009 military strategy review, Obama repeatedly expressed skepticism about pursuing a military solution. So did Vice President Joe Biden and the late Special Envoy Richard Holbrooke. Also dubious of sending more troops were U.S. ambassador and former commanding general in Afghanistan Karl Eikenberry, and the White House "war czar" and senior presidential adviser for Afghanistan, General Douglas Lute. The president told his advisers "I want an exit strategy," according to Bob Woodward's account. "Everything that we're doing has to be focused on how ... we can reduce our military footprint." Yet the strategic review produced a decision to send in 30,000 additional troops. This was fewer than military commanders requested but was a significant increase. "You don't have to do this,"[1] Lute told the president. Having relied primarily on military advice, however, the president received only military options. The thrust of the discussion was not whether to send troops but how many and how fast. This was a sad reflection on the power of the Pentagon to shape presidential decision-making and how war imperatives can trump sound judgment.

This is now Obama's War in the deepest sense. I write this not in anger but with regret and sadness. I admire Obama greatly and support much of his progressive agenda. On this issue, though, the president is ill advised and has placed too much faith in military solutions. The president acknowledged during the strategic review that this is now his war. "I already own it," he said. So do all of us who have supported the president. It is a bitter and tragic irony that the candidate we supported as an advocate for peace has become an architect of war.

Many progressives are reluctant to oppose the president on Afghanistan for fear this will embolden his enemies and undermine his domestic social agenda. I share these concerns and support the president's positive leadership on many issues, but we do the president no favor by remaining silent on a misguided war. We cannot ignore a policy that is diverting vast resources from urgently needed social priorities here at home. The war has become like the "demonic, destructive suction tube" Martin Luther King Jr. envisioned when describing the corrosive effects of the Vietnam War, which eviscerated Lyndon Johnson's war on poverty. The war in Afghanistan has become a voracious machine devouring the dollars and political capital needed to sustain programs for social uplift. It may cripple Obama's domestic reform efforts and could conceivably bring down his presidency. Those who support Obama should be first and strongest in urging a new direction in Afghanistan and in supporting the development of a responsible exit plan.

Demilitarization

When President Obama announced his troop surge in December 2009, he stated that military withdrawals would begin just 18 months later, in July 2011. This coupling of escalation and withdrawal prompted sharp reactions, which ranged from ridicule to disbelief. Why send tens of thousands of additional troops only to remove them soon afterward? To announce a date for withdrawal emboldens enemies and dispirits allies, charged Senator John McCain. Signaling in advance the date of military departure seemed to some like a veiled form of surrender.

In the Afghan context, however, the withdrawal of U.S. and other foreign troops is both wise and necessary. This is the conclusion of the Afghanistan Study Group, a prestigious collection of more than fifty prominent security experts and former government officials who argued in an August 2010 report that the Obama administration should stick firmly to its announced decision to begin withdrawing U.S. troops. The Study Group concurs with the findings of many other foreign policy experts that an overreliance on military solutions has undermined security in Afghanistan. The very presence of American and other foreign troops is a major cause of the insurgency. As the scale of the military intervention has increased, the insurgency has become stronger and the influence of the Taliban has spread. To reverse this perverse dynamic will require a different approach, one that is based on the gradual disengagement of U.S. and NATO military forces.

The United States could immediately improve security and begin to scale back the war by ceasing offensive military operations, particularly commando attacks and night raids on Afghan homes. The number of U.S. military raids has increased significantly with the Obama administration's military surge, and this has created deepening resentment and anger among many Afghans, including President Hamid Karzai. In an interview with the *Washington Post* in November 2010, Karzai said he wanted American troops off the roads and out of Afghan homes. "The time has come to reduce military operations," Karzai said. U.S. troops must cease these raids, he insisted, because they violate the sanctity of Afghan homes and incite more people to join the insurgency.[2] Commanding General David Petraeus reacted with "astonishment and disappointment" to the interview, but Karzai's point is essential. Ending provocative night raids is necessary to improve security and gain the confidence of the Afghan people.

Security in Afghanistan requires fewer foreign troops, not more. Success depends not on additional soldiers, but on better political leaders, more aid workers, and many more educated Afghans—women as well as men. The United States and other countries can and must assist the Afghan people, but we can be most helpful by scaling back and eventually ending our military involvement, combined with greater support for diplomacy, development, and democracy.

This volume makes the case for a calibrated process of military disengagement. It calls for abandoning militarized approaches that have not worked, and ramping up alternative political, diplomatic, and socioeconomic measures that offer greater promise of success. It argues for using the scale and pace of military withdrawals, along with increased spending for development and improved governance, to exert leverage on both the Taliban and the Kabul government. It examines alternative strategies for preventing terrorist insurgency and advancing human rights and development that can be achieved at lower cost and with higher probability of success.

CHAPTER ONE

A "Good War"?

D uring his presidential campaign Barack Obama repeatedly
criticized the Bush administration's policy of invading and
occupying Iraq, but he was equally firm in declaring his support for the U.S. military mission in Afghanistan. In his widely quoted
speech at an antiwar rally in Chicago in October 2002 Obama declared,
"I'm not opposed to all wars. I am opposed to dumb wars." On the
campaign trail in 2008 Obama vowed to end the war in Iraq but said
he would expand military operations in Afghanistan. He criticized the
Bush administration for neglecting Afghanistan and pledged to send
additional U.S. forces to fight al Qaeda and the Taliban. It was thus no
surprise that President Obama expanded the U.S. military commitment
in March and December 2009.

Moral arguments are crucial to the political justification for war in
Afghanistan. President Obama sent more troops to Afghanistan because
he believes this is a just and necessary war and cannot be compared to the
"dumb" policy of invading Iraq. The case for military escalation was made
by journalist Peter Bergen in a 2009 article, "Winning the Good War."
Bergen wrote that Obama's renewed and better-resourced war "will, in
time, produce a relatively stable and prosperous" Afghanistan.[1] Many
experts are less sanguine about the outcome but share the belief in the
necessity of the Afghan mission. Although doubts about the war have
mounted, especially in recent years as military operations have dragged

on inconclusively and casualties have mounted, political opposition has remained relatively muted. Afghanistan has not occasioned anything like the worldwide outcry that greeted George W. Bush's attack on Iraq. Few see viable alternatives to continuing the current policy of military-led counterinsurgency.

Necessity and Choice

The characterization of Afghanistan as a "good war" dates back to the days immediately after 9/11. As the United States prepared to launch strikes in Afghanistan in October 2001, most commentators supported military action as a necessary and legitimate response. The decision to use force and attack the Taliban regime was "certainly a just one," wrote the ethicist Michael Walzer. It was a classic "war of self defense."[2] The U.S. Conference of Catholic Bishops issued a pastoral message acknowledging "the right and duty of a nation and the international community to use military force if necessary to defend the common good by protecting the innocent against mass terrorism."[3] Scott Simon of National Public Radio wrote in the *Wall Street Journal*, "Even Pacifists Must Support This War." In confronting the 9/11 attacks, Simon wrote, there is "no sane alternative now but to support war."[4]

Not everyone was convinced at the time. Although few antiwar protests were mounted in opposition to military operations against the Taliban regime, many religious leaders and peace activists were troubled by the U.S. action. Countering al Qaeda and bringing the 9/11 perpetrators to justice were just purposes, all agreed, but bombing Afghanistan and overthrowing its government seemed questionable methods. Peace advocates argued for a counterterrorism strategy based on cooperative law enforcement rather than war. The proper response to the criminal attacks of al Qaeda was not military invasion, they asserted, but vigorous international police efforts to apprehend perpetrators and prevent future attacks. Reverends Jim Wallis of Sojourners and Bob Edgar of the National Council of Churches circulated a statement among religious leaders appealing for "sober restraint" and warning against indiscriminate retaliation that would cause more loss of innocent life. "Let us deny [the terrorists] their victory by refusing to submit to a world created in their image," the declaration read. The statement was eventually signed by more than 4,000 people and was published in the *New York Times* on November 19, 2001.[5]

Some argued at the time that it was not necessary to overthrow the Taliban-led government, and that alternative diplomatic means were available for isolating al Qaeda and bringing its leaders to justice. An editorial in the Jesuit magazine *America* noted that, although the Afghan government did not accept the Bush administration's ultimatum to turn over Osama bin Laden, Taliban leaders nonetheless offered (1) to negotiate, (2) to put him on trial in an Islamic court, and (3) to turn him over to a third country if the United States provided evidence of his guilt.[6] Two years earlier, when the UN Security Council imposed sanctions against the Taliban regime in response to the bombing of U.S. embassies in Africa, officials in Kabul made similar gestures of diplomatic flexibility. In both instances the United States dismissed the offers as delaying tactics and rejected them as inadmissible legally and unacceptable politically. It is possible, however, that Taliban leaders may have been seeking ways to avoid military attack and distance themselves from bin Laden.[7] In the fall of 1999, as sanctions were about to be enacted, bin Laden wrote a letter to Taliban leader Mullah Muhammad Omar offering to leave Afghanistan. After 9/11 a council of Islamic scholars met and requested that Mullah Omar persuade bin Laden to leave Afghanistan "voluntarily."[8] Some observers believe that Taliban leaders might have been willing to see bin Laden and his terrorist network depart if a graceful exit could have been arranged.[9]

The Bush administration never seriously considered an alternative to war in Afghanistan. According to a *Los Angeles Times* report at the time, "Bush advisors say the president decided from the start he wanted to launch a large-scale military response to the attacks." The White House never veered from that determination and did not pursue diplomatic options for avoiding war. Asked whether Bush ever considered an alternative to military action, National Security Advisor Condoleezza Rice replied firmly, "No."[10] As Duane Shank, senior policy advisor for Sojourners, wrote in the church journal *Mennonite Life*, "Military force was the first resort, not the last."[11] The question of alternatives to military action remains relevant ten years later. In 2011 as in 2001, military means continue to be the primary response rather than a last resort.

Just War Criteria

The question of last resort is important because it is one of the core principles of just war theory. These principles provide a valuable moral framework for deciding when military force may be necessary (*jus ad bellum*) and how it should be used once hostilities are under way (*jus in bello*). They are intended to prevent war, not to make it more permissible. They are challenges to political realism, according to Walzer, and establish strict ethical criteria that must be met before the use of force can be justified.[12] Just war doctrine is based on what the U.S. Catholic Bishops have termed a "presumption *in favor of peace* and *against war*" (emphasis in original). This principle recognizes that war itself is a grave injustice that victimizes the innocent. Overriding the presumption against war requires "extraordinarily strong reasons."[13] War may be a tragic necessity in extreme cases, but it can never be considered virtuous. Theologian Reinhold Niebuhr cautioned against any moral righteousness or attempt to invoke divine sanction for the use of armed force. Killing is always sinful, he argued, even if it is for a just purpose. Wars are conflicts between sinners, not between the righteous and the wicked. They are partly the consequence of our mistaken judgments and imperial policies.[14] The use of force, even if it is deemed necessary, must be undertaken with a deep sense of regret.

Just war principles are often misunderstood and manipulated by powerful interests to justify uses of force that do not meet ethical standards. War is especially unjust when it is waged by powerful states against weak nations and non-state actors in the Global South. When foreign policy is heavily militarized, as in the United States, the use of armed force often becomes a primary response rather than a last resort.[15] In such circumstances war does not meet ethical standards, and the appropriate approach is what philosopher John Rawls termed "contingent pacifism." The possibility of just war is conceded in principle, but the greater likelihood is that war will be unjust.[16]

Self-Defense?

For war to be morally acceptable it must meet strict ethical criteria. Especially important in this case are the principles of just cause, probability of success, and proportionality. Self-defense is the most widely accepted just cause for the use of force. Most religious and moral teachings permit the resort to arms to defend against military aggression. The right of self-defense is acknowledged in many international legal agreements, including the UN Charter. Article 51 of the Charter recognizes the right of states to individual or collective self-defense if an armed attack occurs, but that right is not open ended and exists only "until the Security Council has taken measures necessary to maintain international peace and security." Any military actions taken must be reported to the Security Council and "shall not affect the authority and responsibility of the Security Council" to maintain peace and security. The Charter allows a nation to take immediate action to defend itself but expects that states will then turn to the Security Council to adopt additional measures to ensure peace and security.

The United States did indeed go to the Security Council the day after the 9/11 attacks and received unanimous support for Resolution 1368. That resolution condemned the attacks, recognized the right of self-defense, and expressed the Council's "readiness to take all necessary steps to respond." The Resolution did not authorize any form of military action, however, and was not taken under the authority of Chapter VII of the UN Charter, which is necessary to authorize the use of force. The Council subsequently adopted many resolutions to impose sanctions and other measures against al Qaeda, and to assist with reconstruction and stabilization in post-Taliban Afghanistan, but it never authorized the United States to take "necessary measures" to maintain international peace and security. Washington never requested such authority. It simply bypassed the Council and initiated military strikes unilaterally. It did not provide the required notice to the Security Council and never considered giving the Council responsibility for deciding appropriate security measures.

It is also worth noting that when the United States began military action in October 2001, no continuing terrorist attacks were under way. No evidence was presented or claimed of an imminent threat of additional attacks.[17] This raises further questions about the strategy of using military force. The United States was certainly justified in taking security measures to prevent future terror strikes and bring to justice those responsible for the 9/11 attacks, but was it really necessary to overthrow the Afghan government—and to declare a global "war on terror"? These actions stretched the self-defense argument beyond recognition.

Just Cause

Whether the war in Afghanistan is a just cause depends on the goals of U.S. policy, and whether these can be achieved through military means. The core U.S. objective is defined in the 2010 U.S. National Security Strategy: to "defeat, dismantle, and disrupt" al Qaeda and its violent extremist affiliates in Afghanistan, Pakistan, and beyond. The U.S. Strategy describes Afghanistan and Pakistan as "the epicenter" of al Qaeda violent extremism. It asserts that military pressure is necessary to prevent terrorist attacks on the United States and its allies.[18] Similar arguments were made in the March 2009 White Paper justifying Obama's policy of military buildup. The priority U.S. goal is "disrupting terrorist networks in Afghanistan and especially Pakistan to degrade any ability they have to plan and launch international terrorist attacks."[19] The military mission aims to deny safe havens to al Qaeda and its affiliates and thereby prevent terrorist plots from developing.

The goal of apprehending those responsible for 9/11 and preventing future al Qaeda–related attacks is a just and widely supported cause. Nations have united with rare unanimity and political commitment in recent years to counter the continuing threat to international security posed by mass casualty terror attacks. The goal of preventing such strikes is a morally compelling mission that can be characterized as both self-defense and protection of the innocent. The key ethical and political question is not whether the mission is just, but rather how it can be achieved. It is a question of means rather than ends.

The mission to prevent global terrorist strikes leads to a related objective: building capable governments in Afghanistan and Pakistan that can meet the economic, social, and security needs of their people and provide long-term protection against the use of their territory for international terrorist activity. The administration's White Paper speaks of promoting "a more capable, accountable, and effective government in Afghanistan." It calls for developing "self-reliant Afghan security forces" and assuring a stable government and "vibrant economy" in Pakistan.[20] Again, these are worthy objectives, logically linked to the core mission of preventing global terrorist strikes. The question is one of means rather than ends. Can these worthy goals be met through military means?

From the outset, U.S. military involvement in Afghanistan has been based on three fundamental strategic assumptions: (1) that war and military action are necessary and appropriate means of defeating al Qaeda and preventing global terrorist strikes, (2) that the Taliban is equivalent to al Qaeda and thus a legitimate target of military attack, and (3) that the United States and its allies must fight and win a counterinsurgency war against the Taliban and related jihadist groups. The first two assumptions determined policy decisions in the weeks after 9/11, and they have remained at the heart of U.S./NATO strategy ever since, continuing to shape the direction of military operations. The third assumption underlies the current long-term commitment to military action in the region. All of these assumptions are highly questionable strategically and pose serious dilemmas ethically.

A fourth strategic dimension has entered the equation in recent years—the extension of military operations to Pakistan. U.S. officials view Afghanistan and Pakistan as a single theater of war. Military strategists bemoan Pakistan's role as strategic sanctuary for the insurgency in Afghanistan and worry about spreading Talibanization and armed violence in Pakistan itself. In response Washington has launched commando raids and drone bombing strikes into Pakistan as part of the military mission in Afghanistan. While the armed struggles are linked, the two countries are distinct sovereign entities and must be addressed separately. Whether the United States has legal authority to wage war in Afghanistan is at least arguable, but no such authority exists in the case of Pakistan. The self-defense argument does not apply, since Pakistan was in no way responsible for the 9/11 attacks. Pakistan is designated as a strategic ally of the United States, and its armed forces are engaged in combat operations against Taliban insurgents. Its government has not given formal public consent for U.S. military operations or bombing strikes into its territory. The military attacks into Pakistan have been counterproductive strategically and have dubious legal and ethical justification.

Countering al Qaeda

The al Qaeda threat that originally justified the U.S.-led intervention has changed globally and dwindled in Afghanistan. The al Qaeda brand has spread and been adopted by many Islamist extremist groups around the world, but the operational capability of the old central command in the Afghanistan/Pakistan (Af/Pak) border region has declined. Al Qaeda–related groups have lost ground politically and militarily in some countries, most spectacularly in Iraq, but also in Afghanistan. The al Qaeda movement as a military force has been widely discredited among Muslims around the world and has lost momentum.[21] When an al Qaeda–related group attempted to establish a presence in Gaza it was crushed by Hamas. Al Qaeda's decline has resulted from military and political competition with tribal power structures and revulsion in Muslim communities at the movement's brutal methods and gruesome attacks against civilians. More innocent civilians have been killed by al Qaeda suicide attacks and bombings than by the operations of U.S. troops. While al Qaeda remains a global threat to security, the core organizational structure created by Osama bin Laden has been weakened significantly.

The Afghanistan Study Group noted that there are only some four hundred hardcore al Qaeda fighters in the entire Af/Pak region, with most of them hiding in Pakistan's northwest territories.[22] As the Study Group concludes, the direct U.S. security interests at stake in the Af/Pak region are not sufficient to warrant the massive military commitment involved. No significant al Qaeda presence exists in Afghanistan today, with very little risk of a new safe haven emerging in the future. If the U.S. were to achieve some form of military victory in Afghanistan, this would not affect the capabilities of al Qaeda cells in Somalia, Yemen, and other countries. Nor would it limit the ability of al Qaeda–affiliated groups to threaten terrorist strikes against the United States and key allies. The Study Group concludes that defeating the Taliban, if it were possible, would have little effect on al Qaeda's global reach. The ongoing threat from al Qaeda is better met via specific counterterrorism measures and a reduced U.S. military "footprint" in the Islamic world, according to the Group. War is not necessary or appropriate for this purpose.

CIA director Leon Panetta admitted on ABC News in June 2010 that the total number of al Qaeda terrorists in Afghanistan is "relatively small. At most, we're looking at 50 to 100, maybe less."[23] Many asked in the wake of Panetta's revelation why it is necessary to maintain 100,000 U.S. troops, with tens of thousands of contractors and soldiers from other countries, to wage war against fewer than one hundred fighters. Some also asked why Panetta was offering this information and what political purposes he had in mind. The agency director was touting the presumed success of the administration's continued reliance on CIA drone attacks as a means of decimating the core leadership of al Qaeda. Whatever his motivations, Panetta's comment had the effect of further eroding the justification for large-scale military operations in Afghanistan. If al Qaeda is no longer a substantial force, waging war to destroy it makes even less sense than it did before.

No matter what happens in Afghanistan in the future, the Afghanistan Study Group notes, al Qaeda will not be able to reestablish large training camps and facilities of the sort it employed prior to the 9/11 attacks. The United States and its allies will remain vigilant against al Qaeda while they are withdrawing troops and long afterward. The United States will retain the capability to use air power to destroy any training facilities or operational sites al Qaeda might attempt to create in the region. Any attempt by the bin Laden network to create detectable facilities and military capability would be met with certain and swift military retaliation. The United States and its allies could seek legal and political authority for such action through an International Criminal Court indictment against bin Laden and his lieutenants for crimes against humanity, linked to UN Security Council endorsement of targeted action if they are located. This would strengthen the legal and political foundation for ongoing security measures to suppress al Qaeda. As the Study Group observes, bin Laden and his core team will likely have to remain in hiding the rest of their lives. Al Qaeda will have to continue relying on clandestine cells rather than large encampments or overt military facilities. Covert cells can exist virtually anywhere, including in Europe and North America. Locating and suppressing these threats will remain an ongoing challenge for law enforcement and counterterrorism groups. This struggle will not be affected by the military outcome in Afghanistan, although ending U.S./NATO attacks against Muslim communities there may gradually lower the anger and resentment that feeds jihadist recruitment.

For Women's Rights?

Another frequently mentioned purpose of U.S./NATO policy is protecting and defending the human rights of Afghan women. The Bush administration used the plight of Afghan women as part of its narrative for going to war. On November 17, 2001, in a national radio address, First Lady Laura Bush declared the war against terrorism a fight for the "rights and dignity of women." The aim of liberating Afghan women gradually became a *cause célèbre* for Western feminists and a policy goal of the intervention.

This emphasis on supporting women's rights was more an afterthought than a primary purpose of U.S. military action. In his statement announcing the beginning of military action on October 7, President Bush vowed "sustained, comprehensive, and relentless operations to drive [terrorists] out and bring them to justice." The president also referred to "the oppressed people of Afghanistan," who "would know the generosity" of the United States and its allies. He made no reference to human rights or the plight of women. A month later in a major speech on combating terrorism, Bush described the military mission as "directed at terrorist and military targets" but made no mention of women's rights.[24] A review of statements by senior administration officials in the early weeks of the military operation finds no reference to women's rights. It was not until Laura Bush's November 17 radio address that protecting women's rights emerged as a major theme of U.S. policy.

The emphasis on defending women's rights as a rationale for war has increased in recent years as other justifications have become less convincing. There is evidence that government officials may be using concerns about the plight of Afghan women to build public support for the U.S./NATO military mission. Tucked away in the tens of thousands of pages of WikiLeaks documents released in July 2010 was a recent CIA special memorandum headlined "sustaining West European support for the NATO-led mission" in Afghanistan. The CIA document offers recommendations for shoring up public opinion in the face of growing skepticism in France, Germany, and other European countries. Among the options suggested is the following:

> Afghan women could serve as ideal messengers in humanizing the ISAF role in combating the Taliban because of women's ability to

speak personally and credibly about their experiences under the Taliban, their aspirations for the future, and their fears of a Taliban victory. Outreach initiatives that create media opportunities for Afghan women to share their stories with French, German, and other European women could help to overcome pervasive skepticism among women in Western Europe toward the ISAF mission.[25]

A few days after the WikiLeaks disclosure two major news stories on the travails of Afghan women appeared in the most influential U.S. media. The *New York Times* published a front-page story quoting Afghan women who fear the loss of rights from political reconciliation with the Taliban. The same week *Time* devoted its cover photo and lead story to Aisha, a disfigured eighteen-year-old Afghan girl whose nose was cut off by her husband. The story was headlined "What Happens if We Leave." Aisha was described as frightened by the prospect of political reconciliation with the Taliban and quoted as saying the Taliban "are the people who did this to me."

The attempt to justify war in the name of protecting women's rights is highly questionable. Let's not fool ourselves, writes Nicholas Kristof, that we are doing favors for Afghan women by pursuing an unsustainable war.[26] War is more likely to harm than help women. Women may experience temporary employment gains in the economic stimulus of war, but these are quickly reversed in the downturn and political backlash that often follows. War usually leads to the erosion, not the expansion, of human rights. Civil liberties and personal freedoms are easily sacrificed in the interests of military security. In Afghanistan, Western intervention led initially to an expansion of women's rights, but political backlash and deteriorating security conditions have erased some of the early gains, especially in Taliban-controlled areas. The Afghanistan Study Group asserted that "the worst thing for women is for Afghanistan to remain paralyzed" in war.

Protecting the rights of women in Afghanistan is certainly a just cause, but it is not a justification for invasion and military occupation. The defense of women's rights has been, and should remain, a priority in U.S./NATO policy. It is not a *casus belli*, however. There are many just causes but few just wars. There is no accepted political or ethical principle under just war doctrine that would allow for war or other armed intervention to advance women's rights.

As an occupying military power the United States has a responsibility to protect Afghan civilians. A broad international consensus exists that states have a responsibility to protect innocent civilians. This is embodied in the principle of the Responsibility to Protect (R2P), which has been endorsed by the UN General Assembly and UN Security Council. Some human rights organizations are willing to support the use of force in specific circumstances—if it is necessary to defend persecuted minorities or victimized populations. In the R2P framework armed intervention is to be avoided generally, but extreme circumstances may exist that call for intervention to protect civilians who are victimized by mass violence. Whether these circumstances exist today in Afghanistan is a matter of contention.

The report of the Responsibility to Protect Commission in 2001 developed a rigorous set of principles for determining when and under what conditions humanitarian military intervention could be justified. Military intervention is permissible only in circumstances of violence that genuinely "shock the conscience" or pose a clear and present danger to international security. The commission identified the just cause threshold as actual or anticipated harm involving large-scale loss of life caused by deliberate state action or by ethnic cleansing, killings, forced expulsion, terror, and rape. Only when serious and irreparable harm to large numbers of people occurs is resorting to military force permissible, according to the commission report.[27] The UN Secretary-General's High-level Panel on Threats, Challenges, and Change agreed with these judgments. Its 2004 report endorsed the principle of protective intervention but only "as a last resort, in the event of genocide and other large-scale killing, ethnic cleansing, or serious violations of international humanitarian law."[28]

Women in Afghanistan face severe hardships. Afghan women suffer from innumerable acts of direct and indirect violence at the individual, family, and social level. The death toll from this violence is impossible to quantify, except for the numbers of those killed and injured by insurgency and war. Whether this qualifies as "mass killing" is a matter of judgment. The greatest loss of life results from the insurgency and counterinsurgency. Women also suffer injury and death from the violence perpetrated by husbands and family members, by armed men who rape and exploit them sexually, and by roving bands of Taliban religious fanatics who attack them because of their behavior or beliefs. They die and suffer more often from the indirect violence of early unattended childbirth, lack of medical care and sanitation, poor nutrition, and the many threats to health and well-being that exist in their war-ravaged and undeveloped society. Many die a slow death of lost fulfillment and illiteracy, burdened with constant childbearing and homemaking, virtually imprisoned behind the closed doors of their male-dominated households. These harsh realities constitute very real forms of direct and indirect violence. Are they comparable, though, to the threats of genocidal killing and large-scale loss of life that have been identified as conditions for military intervention?

Even if we find that the scale of torment for Afghan women is sufficiently large to warrant the costs and risks of continued military occupation, the problem arises of identifying the perpetrators and targeting military pressure in a manner that ends the suffering. Clearly many Taliban fighters and supporters are misogynists and are guilty of having injured, raped, and killed women. But which Taliban members are responsible for these crimes, and what specific action should be taken against them? Is it appropriate to target an entire insurgent movement, including young recruits who may have had no involvement in such acts, because of the offenses of some?

The problem of misogyny in Afghanistan is not confined to the Taliban, although they may be most zealous and cruel. Many of the warlords and former mujahideen who are part of the Karzai government have engaged in similar practices and have similar beliefs. During their rule in the 1990s, the mujahideen were extremely brutal and repressive toward women. Some are guilty like the Taliban of having injured and killed women. These strongmen now sit in Parliament, govern provinces, command security forces, and direct elements of the Afghan government. If the crime to be punished is the oppression of women, pressure will need to be applied against a large portion of the Afghan male population, including members of the current Afghan government.

Questioning the ethical argument for war does not mean condoning or accepting Taliban policies, which are utterly repugnant and contrary to cherished principles of freedom and human rights. A moral and political obligation exists to stem the spread of extremist influence and protect the rights of women of Afghanistan. These goals cannot be met through military means, however, and the attempt to do so through large-scale foreign intervention has failed thus far and has had the unintended effect of arousing greater insurgency and extremism. The pursuit of political reconciliation and a negotiated solution offer viable alternatives. The best way to work for the rights of Afghan women is through political means, persuasion, and patient dialogue (the proverbial three cups of tea), not war and military coercion.

Avoiding Civilian Casualties

As insurgency and war have intensified in Afghanistan in recent years, the number of civilian deaths and injuries has increased significantly, especially in southern Pashtun communities. According to the UN Assistance Mission in Afghanistan (UNAMA) the total number of recorded civilian deaths in 2009 was 2,412. This was an increase of 14 percent over the 2,118 civilian deaths recorded in 2008. In the first half of 2010, deaths and injuries increased further, with 1,271 civilians killed and nearly 2,000 injured. This was a 31 percent increase over the comparable period a year earlier, before the Obama surge.[29] Civilian casualties have risen to their highest level since UNAMA began systematically documenting these figures in 2007.[30] Aggregate data indicate that at least 9,400 Afghan civilians were killed in conflict-related hostilities from 2006 through fall 2010.[31] To these figures must be added the hundreds of civilian casualties that have resulted from U.S. bombing raids in Pakistan. These numbers are not as high as the horrendous civilian death tolls in other conflicts, such as Iraq and Darfur, but any loss of innocent life is significant and affects the political and moral calculus of war.

According to UNAMA estimates, more than 70 percent of civilian casualties are caused by the actions of insurgent forces, mostly from the effects of improvised explosive devices (IEDs), car bombings, suicide attacks, and assaults against foreign troops and their Afghan supporters. Casualties also have been caused by Afghan government and U.S./ NATO forces, although the percentages are much lower. Civilian deaths from these forces are caused by air strikes, drone attacks, and military operations, as well as so-called "escalation of force" incidents in which civilians are fired upon at checkpoints or near military convoys.

Civilian casualties are poisonous to a counterinsurgency campaign that hopes to win hearts and minds. When civilians are killed by U.S./ NATO forces, family and community members tend to seek revenge and may join or support the insurgency. Military doctrine tries to avoid this dilemma through a counterinsurgency strategy that is "population-centric." The focus of this approach is not killing the maximum number of enemy fighters but protecting the civilian population from harm and competing with insurgent forces for influence at the grassroots level. A population-centric strategy seeks to create conditions for human security. "The aim should be not to arrest or kill adversaries," writes Pentagon adviser David Kilcullen, "but to co-opt them—not to destroy the enemy but to win him over."[32] The most successful programs are those that work with communities to address the underlying conditions that terrorists exploit.

Civilian casualties are also a challenge to the moral basis of war, particularly to the ethical standards of proportionality and discrimination. According to just war doctrine the lives lost in warfare must be proportionate to the good expected to result. The presumed political and security gains from military action must be sufficient to justify the resulting human suffering. Ethical guidelines require that soldiers discriminate between combatants and civilians and avoid harming the innocent. Under the principle of double effect, the harm that may result from seeking good must not be intended nor serve as a means to an end. According to Walzer's interpretation of this principle, the soldier must take positive action to minimize the evil effect, and be prepared to accept costs for doing so.[33]

Senior U.S./NATO commanders have acknowledged the need to reduce civilian casualties and have sought ways to avoid what they consider collateral damage or unintended consequences. One of the most important steps in this regard has been the decision to limit the use of indiscriminate military force. In June 2009 Commanding General Stanley McChrystal issued directives restricting the use of force in populated areas and reducing the number of U.S. air strikes in support of combat missions.[34] In the spring of 2010 NATO officials even considered the idea of creating a medal for "courageous restraint," which would be awarded to soldiers who take risks to avoid harming civilians. The proposal for a military restraint medal would make sense for ethicists, but it generated a firestorm of ridicule and rebuke among military traditionalists and was quietly dropped. It is hard to convince soldiers who are trained to use firepower that they should restrain that force in the midst of combat.

The Taliban also issued a code of conduct to prevent civilian casualties in July 2009, but the total number of civilian deaths attributed to insurgent forces rose that year by 41 percent compared with 2008.[35] Mullah Omar and other Taliban leaders have condemned the use of suicide terror tactics that kill innocent civilians, urging fighters to focus their attacks on foreign troops and Afghan government forces, but insurgent methods are inherently indiscriminate and inevitably kill many innocent, unprotected bystanders.[36]

Evidence suggests that estimates of civilian casualties caused by U.S.-led military operations may be understated. The WikiLeaks documents indicate that U.S. and allied strikes have caused many more civilian deaths than officially acknowledged. Claimed insurgent casualties often include civilian deaths. An analysis of 2008 casualty figures by the independent organization Afghanistan Rights Monitor found that some of the alleged 1,700 insurgents killed that year were actually civilians wrongly labeled as enemy combatants.[37] U.S./NATO officials also understate the number of civilian casualties resulting from their actions. Analyst Antonio Giustozzi examined figures from 2006 and found that actual civilian casualties were higher than NATO/U.S. estimates. In the few cases investigated, "Civilian casualties were regularly reported to be higher than initial NATO/U.S. estimates."[38] The extent of such reporting errors is unknown, but total numbers of civilian fatalities likely are higher than officially recorded.

In the counterinsurgency war being fought in Afghanistan, noncombatant casualties are likely to continue, despite NATO efforts to avoid them. Upholding standards of civilian immunity is extremely difficult in this type of struggle, because irregular combatants do not wear uniforms and often mix with or are part of the civilian population. This is "war amongst the people," to use the phrase of former British general Rupert Smith. Ordinary people inevitably suffer in such a conflict. U.S. and NATO officials have not fully addressed the moral and strategic consequences of this persistent dilemma.

How (Not) to Counter Terrorism

Al Qaeda's attack on the United States was a politically motivated criminal act by international conspirators. It was not an act of war. The terrorist strikes were of monstrous proportions—killing nearly 3,000 people, striking the power centers of the world's mightiest nation, and sending shock waves of fear and horror across the globe—but they were mounted by a non-state organization, not another government. Waging war to counter such a threat is inappropriate, wrote Catholic ethicist Reverend J. Bryan Hehir. "Containing and capturing terrorists is by definition a function of police and legal networks. War is an indiscriminate tool for this highly discriminating task."[39] Most governments and international officials have consistently emphasized the necessity of effective law enforcement to counter terrorism. The head of the Crown Prosecution Service in the United Kingdom said, "The fight against terrorism on the streets of Britain is not a war. It is the prevention of crime, the enforcement of our laws, and the winning of justice for those damaged by their infringement."[40]

Al Qaeda is a transnational network of terrorists committed to perpetrating acts of mass murder. It is also a movement that has spread like cancer within Muslim communities throughout the world. The militants who take up the al Qaeda cause certainly have the capability to inflict casualties, but they are not a threat to state power. The organization lacks substantial armed forces and does not pose a threat to the existence or military capability of the United States or any other major state. Osama bin Laden and his disciples are "small men and secondary threats whose shadows are made large" by our exaggerated fears, writes veteran CIA analyst Glenn Carle. Al Qaeda's "capabilities are far inferior to its desires."[41] Bin Laden has vowed to wage war on the United States and overthrow corrupt Arab governments, but his organization has never had the faintest capability of achieving such megalomaniacal purposes. To believe otherwise, as many U.S. officials apparently did in the days after 9/11, was to give credence to bin Laden's pretense. It legitimized his claim to global leadership and played into his hands.[42] To declare the campaign against al Qaeda a "war on terror" was to give military status to a criminal organization. It transformed mass murderers into soldiers, inadvertently raising their credibility and moral stature in some Muslim communities.

Empirical evidence indicates that war is not an effective means of countering terrorist organizations. A 2008 RAND Corporation study, *How Terrorist Groups End,* shows that terrorist groups usually end through political processes and effective law enforcement, not the use of military force. An examination of 268 terrorist organizations that ended during a period of nearly forty years found that the primary factors accounting for their demise were participation in political processes (43 percent) and effective policing (40 percent). Military force accounted for the end of terrorist groups in only 7 percent of the cases examined. Terrorist groups end most often when they adopt nonviolent means and join a political process or when local law enforcement agencies arrest or kill key members. Policing works better than war because law enforcement officials are rooted in local communities, and they can gain the knowledge and trust of local residents that enables them to penetrate terrorist networks.[43] Political bargaining and accommodation are most common when terrorist groups have localized rather than global objectives. Al Qaeda has a millenarian agenda and is not susceptible to political compromise. Many Taliban fighters, however, are focused narrowly on removing foreign forces from their communities, which suggests that they might be amenable to negotiation if that goal can be met.

Blowback

War policies are not only inappropriate; they are counterproductive. The use of large-scale military operations to counter terrorism has had significant negative consequences. The invasion and occupation of Iraq generated what conservative analyst Francis Fukuyama termed a "frenzy of anti-Americanism" around the world.[44] Al Qaeda and related extremist groups experienced a significant boost in recruitment and political support in response to the invasion and occupation of Iraq. While the hostility toward U.S. policy has ebbed slightly under the Obama administration, and al Qaeda–related militancy has diminished in Iraq, the recruitment of jihadi extremists has risen sharply in Afghanistan and Pakistan.

The policies of waging war in Muslim countries have the unintended effect of validating bin Laden's warped ideology of saving Islam from foreign infidels. When the United States invades and occupies Muslim countries, this undermines our moral standing and validates the false image of America waging war on Islam. A widely accepted narrative now pervades much of the world. It is a story of illegal invasions; abuse at Abu Ghraib and other prisons; torture, water boarding, and extrajudicial killings; drones raining terror from the sky—all continuously broadcast by Arab and Muslim media. This tale of American perfidy is reinforced every time the United States kills civilians or engages in other acts that are seen as reprehensible. Polls in Muslim countries have shown 80 percent agreement with bin Laden's contention that American policy is directed against Islamic society, that the United States is waging war against Islam itself.[45] As long as these attitudes prevail there will be no end of recruits willing to blow themselves up to kill Americans and their supporters.

President Obama declared during his address in Cairo in June 2009 that "America is not—and never will be—at war with Islam." His administration ended the use of the phrase "war on terror" and has emphasized civilian means of overcoming violent extremism. These are positive developments that may begin to mitigate the corrosive impacts of previous policies, but the tone of the administration has not been matched by substantive changes on the ground. U.S. policies and commitments in the Af/Pak region remain heavily militarized and have become more so with the addition of tens of thousands of troops. The Obama administration may have discontinued "war on terror" language but many of the past policies continue. A war on terror by another name.

The greatest threat to U.S. security is not al Qaeda itself but the misguided strategy of countering terrorism with military means. The supposed cure of waging war against terrorism is "worse than the disease," writes Kilcullen.[46] U.S. war policies, and the resistance they engender, have caused far greater loss of life and destruction than the original al Qaeda attacks. The policy of large-scale Western military intervention in Iraq and Afghanistan has led to the death and injury of tens of thousands of civilians and thousands of U.S. troops. It has drained the U.S. Treasury of more than one trillion dollars and eroded international respect and support for American leadership. It has unleashed a war without borders, without limits, and potentially without end.[47]

Military intervention in Muslim countries is a trap. It is exactly what Islamist extremists want. Al Qaeda seeks to bleed intervening forces to exhaustion and bankruptcy, while counting on their military overreaction to arouse public anger and generate recruits for further armed resistance. As Kilcullen observes, "our too-willing and heavy-handed interventions in the so-called war on terrorism to date have largely played into the hands" of this exhaustion strategy, while creating tens of thousands of Taliban recruits and "tying us down in a costly (and potentially unsustainable) series of interventions."[48] The American military has allowed itself to become bogged down in a form of asymmetric warfare that benefits the adversary while canceling U.S. advantages.

The Rejection Response

Many observers of the current conflict have concluded that the presence of foreign troops is a principal cause of armed resistance and insurgency in the region. A report of the Carnegie Endowment for International Peace in 2009 observed, "The more military pressure is put on a fragmented society like Afghanistan, the more a coalition against the invader becomes the likely outcome." The presence of foreign troops is "the most important factor in mobilizing support for the Taliban."[49] Graham Fuller, former CIA station chief in Kabul, wrote: "Occupation everywhere creates hatred, as the U.S. is learning." Although few Pashtuns support bin Laden's global agenda, many are willing to ally themselves with the insurgent war against the U.S. military.[50]

Kilcullen uses a medical analogy to describe what he terms the "rejection response." In communities subjected to invasion and occupation there is an immune reaction in which the body "rejects the intrusion of a foreign object." When the United States sends combat forces to control countries like Iraq and Afghanistan, this creates an "antibody response" in the form of armed insurgency. The effect of intrusive military actions on political stability in affected communities is entirely negative. This is especially so in response to punitive raiding and the use of airstrikes. In the face of outside intervention local groups coalesce in a fusion response, closing ranks against the external threat. This reaction is lessened if the intervention is lower profile and less violent, but a large-scale, violent, foreign-based intervention tends to increase support for local terrorist groups.

The rejection phenomenon can also be described as an "occupation effect," a predictable political-military reaction that occurs when external military forces attempt to dominate a hostile or unwilling population. This is a general rule of politics in response to coercive intervention. It is akin to the "rally 'round the flag effect." When faced with an unwanted foreign intruder, people naturally tend to come together to resist. In doing so they may support an extremist movement not because they endorse its ideology, but because that movement has taken the lead in organizing opposition to foreign occupation. People in societies under attack naturally tend to side with local rather than external forces, with co-religionists rather than those of other faiths. They support and join insurgent forces because they are mobilized to support local interests or are alienated by heavy-handed actions of the outside forces. When Afghan civilians are subjected to wrongful arrest and harassment, when they face violations of the privacy of their homes and affronts to the dignity of women, they are more likely to engage in armed resistance.[51]

Kilcullen has written of the "accidental guerrilla" phenomenon. The accidental guerrilla is one who fights outsiders because they are intruding into his space. Local insurgents "fight us not because they seek our destruction but because they believe we seek theirs." The foot soldiers of the Afghan insurgency are seeking to drive out foreign military invaders, not to reinstate the caliphate or advance al Qaeda's globalist agenda. It is not religious extremism or support for Taliban ideology that motivates support for the insurgency, but rather the anger and desire for revenge that result from wrongful killing and destruction by U.S.-led and Afghan government forces.[52] The larger and more destructive the military force arrayed against targeted communities, the greater the armed resistance.[53] This phenomenon is developing in Pakistan as well, where U.S. military operations and drone strikes are driving many Pashtuns into the arms of Taliban extremists.[54]

Empirical studies indicate a link between military occupation and suicide terrorist attacks. Studies by Robert Pape and other scholars show that opposition to military occupation is a major factor driving suicide terrorism. Nearly all the political scientists and sociologists who have studied the phenomenon agree that suicide attacks are linked to struggles against military occupation.[55] Pape's database includes more than 2,000 suicide attacks from 1983 to the present and shows a strong association between the presence of foreign military forces and the rise of such attacks. His analysis confirms that military occupation is the main factor driving suicide terrorism.[56] Most suicide terror attacks occur as part of organized campaigns to compel the withdrawal of foreign military forces from territory that the terrorists consider to be their homeland. A 2006 report by UN secretary-general Kofi Annan came to similar conclusions: "suicide terrorism campaigns often occur in the context of foreign occupation or perceived foreign occupation."[57] Whether in Kashmir, Chechnya, Palestine, Iraq, or Afghanistan, suicide bombings have a common purpose and political agenda: to drive out what are seen as foreign occupation forces.

In quelling terrorist insurgency, outside military forces are the problem, not the solution. This is the paradox of U.S. military power in Afghanistan and Pakistan. The greater involvement of U.S. and other foreign forces has not produced greater security, but has led to increased violence and a weakening of government authority and legitimacy. The very presence of U.S. forces has sparked terrorism and armed resistance.

A Legitimate Role for Security Forces

The critique of war as a strategy for countering terrorism does not mean that military force has no role to play in Afghanistan and Pakistan. Nor is it an argument for precipitous troop withdrawals that could further undermine security and strengthen extremist forces. Demilitarization is necessary to help stabilize the region and reduce armed violence, but the process of U.S. military disengagement must be gradual and should be linked to parallel diplomatic efforts and alternative security arrangements. Protection is needed for civilians who perform development and peace-building tasks, and for tribal leaders and civil society activists who stand up against extremism. Teachers and students may also need protection. Such missions should be provided wherever possible by local forces, but an interim Muslim-led security force also may be necessary, as outlined below. As they begin to withdraw, U.S. and NATO units should assist in equipping the interim security force and should continue to provide training and equipment to Afghan forces.[58]

If force is to be used, it should be constrained, narrowly targeted against known criminals, and applied within the context of law enforcement rather than military combat. Policing is distinct from and ethically more justifiable than war.[59] Political scientist Robert Johansen has proposed ways to use international courts and multilateral policing to achieve justice and protect the innocent while strengthening the rule of law.[60] These approaches, when combined with cooperative law enforcement and intelligence sharing among governments, are effective means of reducing the operational capacity of terrorist networks. They are ethically and operationally superior to war as means of countering terrorist insurgency.

Cooperative law enforcement has been and remains one of the most effective tools for countering terrorist networks. In the weeks after 9/11 the United States worked bilaterally with many countries and multilaterally through the UN Security Council to establish a global counterterrorism program that focused on law enforcement cooperation and the denial of financial assets and other forms of support for al Qaeda and its supporters.[61] This "invisible war" against terrorism has had significant results. In the months after the attacks, hundreds of suspected terrorists were arrested, and tens of millions of dollars in alleged terrorist financial assets were frozen. These efforts, which have continued to the present, have impeded al Qaeda operations and impaired its ability to launch terrorist strikes.[62] Multilateral police action has been successful in thwarting many terrorist attacks. In August 2006 British law enforcement and intelligence officials cooperated with their counterparts in Pakistan and the United States to interdict plots against flights from London to U.S. cities that could have killed thousands. The reports of the Center on Global Counterterrorism Cooperation have documented a wide range of practical policy options for improving global counterterrorism efforts. These options are far more effective than military action in suppressing and defending against the threat of terrorist violence.

CHAPTER TWO

An Unwinnable War

P robability of success is an important criterion in just war doctrine, requiring that military force not be used in a futile cause or in circumstances where disproportionate force would be needed to assure success. Many analysts have raised doubts about the ability of the United States and its allies to achieve military victory in the current struggle. General Sir David Richards, chief of the British defense staff, recently told an interviewer for the Sunday *Telegraph* that insurgency in Afghanistan cannot be defeated.[1] Afghanistan's reputation as the graveyard of empires is well earned and based on a long history of fierce and often successful resistance to foreign military intervention, most strikingly in the defeat of the Soviet occupation of 1979–1989. A similar pattern of resistance has emerged now in the Pashtun regions of the country and in northwest Pakistan. General David Petraeus has acknowledged that the United States and its allies are up against "an industrial strength insurgency," one that cannot be defeated through purely military means. The meager results so far of more than nine years of U.S./NATO combat operations reinforce doubts about military viability.

Counterinsurgency to the Rescue?

U.S. officials pin their hopes for success on the effective implementation of the principles of counterinsurgency warfare, COIN in military shorthand. The study of counterinsurgency has become a major priority in recent years. The Defense Department under Donald Rumsfeld initially denied the existence of insurgency in Iraq and Afghanistan, but the hard realities of war forced a reevaluation. Since 2004–2005, interest in counterinsurgency has expanded sharply. The production of studies on the subject has become a cottage industry.

According to the official U.S. State Department guide, counterinsurgency is "primarily a political struggle." It seeks to reinforce the legitimacy of local government while reducing insurgent influence. This often requires political reform to improve the quality of governance and address legitimate political grievances.

> The political function is the key function, providing a framework of political reconciliation, and reform of governance around which all other COIN activities are organized. In general, a COIN strategy is only as good as the political plan at its heart.[2]

Military specialists have long recognized that counterinsurgency is primarily a civilian task. The classic military book on the subject by David Galula calls for a struggle that is 80 percent nonmilitary.[3] The U.S. Army's 2006 counterinsurgency field manual, coauthored by Petraeus, echoes this classic emphasis on prioritizing civilian efforts and repeats the call for a struggle that is mostly nonmilitary.

The U.S. mission in Afghanistan is exactly the opposite. A May 2009 Congressional Research Service study reports that some 94 percent of all U.S. funds for the wars in Afghanistan and Iraq have been spent by the Pentagon, with only 6 percent devoted to foreign aid and diplomatic operations. In Afghanistan military operations have received by far the largest share of U.S. funding, $224 billion through mid-2009.

Reconstruction and civil programs in Afghanistan received just $38 billion, with much of that channeled through the Pentagon for training and arming Afghan security forces.[4]

The U.S. military strategy in Afghanistan is seriously flawed, according to Karl Eide, the former head of the UN mission in Afghanistan. In a January 2010 interview as he was leaving office, Eide criticized the military surge ordered by President Obama and argued that the military campaign in Afghanistan "is doomed to failure" without major changes. The focus must be on political solutions, he argued, but this has been subordinated to an increased emphasis on combat operations. "The strategy has to be demilitarized," Eide asserted, and must be based on a "meaningful, Afghan-led political strategy."[5]

The plan for U.S. military success in Afghanistan is based on the Petraeus policy of "clear, build, and hold." U.S. forces enter a community, drive out insurgent forces, establish a long-term security presence, build reconstruction projects, provide humanitarian and development aid, and hold on until local authorities have the capabilities and governance capacity to maintain control.[6] This is the approach that supposedly brought success and a reduction of violence in Iraq.

As Antonio Giustozzi has noted, the strategy of long-term occupation and pacification is impossible to apply consistently across a country as large as Afghanistan. Occupying one area leaves other portions of the country open to the insurgents, who can travel freely or lie low until the foreign forces move on. The task of permanently controlling territory is supposed to be the job of the Afghan security forces, but clearly they are not up to the task. It is highly unlikely, according to Giustozzi, that U.S. military action can defeat the insurgents.[7] Counterinsurgency strategy might have worked better in the early days of the insurgency, before it spread, but once the Taliban became active in many districts, it was no longer possible to provide sufficient troops and development funding to control the vast areas required.

Eide offered a similar critique of the Petraeus doctrine. It is not possible to clear when opponents are insurgents one day and normal villagers the next. To hold requires a lengthy process of facilitating the emergence of accountable police and governance structures at the local level. Efforts to build are not feasible if development agencies are made accomplices of an unpopular foreign military intervention. Genuine progress toward development and governance will not be possible, according to Eide, without greater respect for Afghanistan's religion, culture, and traditions.

Flawed Implementation

In August 2009 Commanding General Stanley McChrystal conducted a reassessment of U.S./NATO strategy that called for a greater emphasis on population protection. The focus should be on engaging and protecting the population, McChrystal asserted, not seizing territory or killing insurgents.[8] The McChrystal strategy has not been implemented effectively, however. Military commanders have continued to emphasize combat operations and the destruction of Taliban forces. Western officials have focused on the goal of defeating the Taliban and al Qaeda rather than enhancing the safety and security of the Afghan people.

U.S. leaders have reverted to the practice, discredited during the Vietnam era, of defining military progress according to the number of dead insurgents. In 2002 Commanding General Tommy Franks had said "we don't do body counts,"[9] but more recently military officials have claimed success by touting the number of insurgents killed. In a counterinsurgency struggle this is tantamount to an admission of failure. Unable to cite evidence for the most important indicator of success, growing support for the Afghan government, officials fall back on the practice of measuring death as the standard of progress.

Analysts Marika Theros and Mary Kaldor recently conducted interviews with civil society actors in Afghanistan and found that the emphasis on combat is undermining security. The greatest insecurity in Afghanistan exists in areas where U.S.-led forces conduct military operations. Western offensives and Taliban counteroffensives produce violence and civilian suffering. Even where civilian casualties are avoided, people are often displaced, and homes and villages are damaged or destroyed. The result is often greater animosity toward external forces and increased support for armed resistance.

Theros and Kaldor focus on what they describe as "the extremely inflammatory practice of night raids on Afghan homes." Many Afghans consider this the single biggest factor feeding the insurgency. An Open Society Institute investigation found similar public outrage against night raids.[10] The Theros and Kaldor account deserves citation:

> Soldiers break into homes, rough up men, women and children, and frequently detain family members for weeks or months without accountability. This would be unacceptable in any Western country; in traditional societies it breaks every cultural taboo violating the integrity and sanctity of the home and women. Even the Soviets were more sophisticated. As one respondent from Khost starkly put it, "The Soviets killed us by bombing us, but they did not come into our homes, disrespect our women, and kill our families." Additionally, most Afghans believe these raids are provoked by informers seeking to settle personal scores.[11]

U.S. commanders have attempted to adopt a more civilian-oriented approach, but the war paradigm remains ascendant. Despite the stated strategy of engaging Afghan civilians, military objectives continue to dominate both rhetoric and practice. The goal of helping to create a more secure and democratic Afghan society has been sacrificed to military imperatives.

Factors of Failure

Of the numerous recent reports on counterinsurgency doctrine, one of the most authoritative and compelling is the RAND Corporation's 2008 study *War by Other Means*. The study examines historical examples to identify the core factors that account for the success or failure of counterinsurgency operations. Once an insurgency reaches large scale, as in Afghanistan, COIN missions have a 50 percent chance of success, which means they fail half the time. The specific circumstances of the war in Afghanistan increase the likelihood of failure. According to the study, "four of the strongest statistical predictors of successful insurgency" are all prevalent in the Muslim world generally and in Afghanistan specifically. These are as follows:

- populations excluded from politics and estranged from the state
- authoritarian, unresponsive, inept, and corrupt government
- insurgents committed to destroying such government
- significant popular sympathy for insurgents

All these conditions exist in Afghanistan today, and make the probability of counterinsurgency success less than 50 percent.

Another major factor contributing to the failure of counterinsurgency is, ironically, the involvement of large numbers of foreign troops. The presence of foreign forces is usually an indicator of failure. Here again the paradox of counterinsurgency: more troops means less security. When an insurgency reaches the point where large-scale foreign intervention is needed to prop up the state, the cause is usually already lost. The study's conclusion on this point bears full citation:

> History provides no basis for expecting large-scale foreign military intervention to make COIN victorious. Rather, there is a correlation between large-scale foreign military intervention and unsuccessful COIN. The larger the foreign troop presence—France in Algeria, France and the United States in Indochina, the USSR in Afghanistan—the worse the outcome tends to be.[12]

The military historian Martin van Creveld explains why attempts to suppress insurgency usually end in failure. When guerrilla forces are able to maintain armed struggle for prolonged periods, often for decades, they are able to prevail over stronger and more technologically advanced adversaries.[13] The occupying forces may win every battle and destroy much of the insurgent capability, yet in the long run the guerrilla forces usually win. The rare examples of counterinsurgency success, van Creveld argues, come when intervening forces are willing to wage war with unrestrained cruelty and destructiveness, as exemplified by Nazi suppression of partisan resistance in much of occupied Europe. Fortunately the U.S. military does not fight in that manner. On the contrary, U.S. and NATO forces are subject to democratic constraint and as a result are unlikely to be able to sustain the prolonged large-scale militarily destructive effort that would be required for success. Already several NATO countries have developed plans to reduce their military presence in Afghanistan. It is doubtful that American taxpayers and the U.S. Congress will be willing to sustain the required sacrifice in terms of lives lost and resources spent for the additional years military officials say is necessary. All of these factors make the probability of success uncertain at best.

Counterinsurgency experts cite successful British experiences in defeating insurgents in Malaya, Kenya, Oman, and Borneo. As Giustozzi notes, however, analysts overlook the main factor in securing those victories, which was the British preference for political solutions rather than wars that could not be won. The celebrated victories were made possible by London's willingness to compromise and abandon control of territory, in exchange for assurances that vital British interests would be protected.[14]

Success in counterinsurgency missions often requires narrowing the objectives and engaging in dialogue with adversaries. The United States has tended to take an opposite approach. Rather than narrowing the focus and seeking political compromise, U.S. leaders have elevated the importance of the fight and refused to talk to the adversary. In the process they have unwittingly trapped themselves in a situation that limits their strategic and tactical flexibility.

In January 2010 Andrew J. Enterline and Joseph Magagnoli at the University of North Texas completed an empirical study on all major insurgencies fought around the world since 1946. Their analysis shows that counterinsurgency campaigns result in military victory about half the time. This confirms the RAND analysis. That's the good news for counterinsurgents. The bad news is that all of the indicators of likely failure are present in Afghanistan.

Counterinsurgency campaigns fail if they do not shift quickly from enemy-centric to population-centric strategies. That shift did not come for the United States in Afghanistan until 2009, nearly eight years into the campaign. It would take years of additional military effort to achieve gains in population-centric policies, a prospect Enterline and Magagnoli call "daunting given the marked erosion of American and allied public support for continued war in Afghanistan." Counterinsurgency campaigns also tend to fail when they are waged by heavily armed, technologically advanced armies. This turns one of the presumed strengths of the U.S. military into a liability. Guerrilla forces rely on local populations for support, while industrialized armies must be supplied from their home countries. Outside forces lack the natural connections with local communities that make it easier to win hearts and minds and obtain effective intelligence about insurgents. These and other factors reduce the prospects of success. The authors conclude that in light of these factors the prospect of achieving military victory in Afghanistan "approaches zero."[15]

The Iraq Surge as a Model?

When the Obama administration decided to increase U.S. troop levels in Afghanistan, many analysts pointed to the claimed success of the surge policy in Iraq as a precedent. The addition of approximately 30,000 extra U.S. troops in 2007 was credited with bringing about a dramatic reduction in violence in Iraq. Proponents of a surge in Afghanistan argued for a similar approach. Following the surge script in Iraq, officials asserted, would increase the chances of military success in Afghanistan.

The Iraq surge policy is not a viable model, however. The consensus among leading military and security analysts is that the Iraq troop surge was not the primary or sole factor responsible for the reduction of violence in Iraq in 2007 and 2008. Other developments were more important in changing military dynamics in Iraq. According to scholar Colin Kahl, the surge was only one of four interrelated factors that helped to improve the security situation.[16] The other three factors were the Awakening movement among Iraqi Sunnis, the cease-fire by the Shiite Mahdi Army of Muqtada al-Sadr, and what Steve Simon called "the grim success of ethnic cleansing." The battles among armed Iraqi factions for control of neighborhoods in Baghdad and other cities were largely concluded by 2008, leading to the creation of segregated and heavily defended sectarian enclaves.[17] The surge was not the decisive factor in quelling insurgent violence in Iraq and thus hardly qualifies as a model for achieving similar results in Afghanistan.

The decision of Sunni sheiks to turn against al Qaeda was particularly important in stemming the Iraqi insurgency. This revolt was initiated entirely by the Sunni tribes.[18] The revolt that became the Awakening movement began in 2006, months before the troop surge was even considered and well before additional U.S. troops began to arrive. The Anbar Salvation Council was formed by Sunni sheiks in September 2006.[19] Its creation was sparked by the actions of various Sunni tribal leaders, warlords, insurgents, and militants who decided to turn against their former al Qaeda allies.

The Sunni groups were reacting to al Qaeda's power grabs, executions, and encroachments into tribal leadership and tradition.[20] Groups such as al Qaeda in Iraq attempted to forcibly assimilate local tribal militias and impose strict Sharia practices within traditionally secular Sunni communities. Al Qaeda militants assassinated or killed in firefights some thirty local commanders of tribal militias as part of their power grab in al Anbar district.[21] The militants also violated local custom by demanding to marry the daughters of local sheiks, seeking to establish political/military alliances through intermarriage. These and other al Qaeda abuses backfired and created deepening resentment and resistance among the sheiks and their militia members.

The Sunni tribal leaders were also motivated by concerns about their growing political marginalization in Iraq and the rise of a Shia-dominated government in Baghdad. Previously accustomed to political predominance and privilege, Sunni leaders now found themselves isolated and weakened in the emerging new Iraqi state. Faced with these twin threats to their way of life—externally from al Qaeda, internally from the rise of Shia power—the sheiks began to cooperate with their former enemies in the U.S. military and rose up in revolt against al Qaeda. By March 2007, as the additional U.S. troops began to arrive, the political and military transformation of al Anbar was already mostly complete.[22]

The Awakening movement brought 95,000 Iraqis into alliance with U.S. forces. Without this decisive shift in the military balance, the security gains in Iraq "would have been completely impossible," according to Kilcullen.[23] The tribes in the Awakening movement were not pro-American, much less pro-government, but they were strongly anti–al Qaeda. The Sunni tribes decided to side with the United States to advance their own sectarian agenda and strengthen their political standing in advance of U.S. military withdrawal. Their alliance with American forces was purely a matter of convenience and did not reflect loyalty to what the United States was attempting to achieve in Iraq.[24]

Battling the Taliban

U.S./NATO strategy equates the goal of countering al Qaeda with defeating the Taliban insurgency. The original decision to overthrow the Taliban regime in 2001 was based on this assumption, and current policy remains wedded to it. This assessment is crucial to the current military mission, since nearly all U.S. military action in the region is directed at the Taliban. Al Qaeda has only a marginal role in the military action taking place in Afghanistan.[25] The U.S./NATO military operation is primarily a war against the Taliban, not al Qaeda. This alters the moral and political calculus and casts doubt on the assertion of self-defense as a justification for war.

Al Qaeda and the Taliban have been closely intertwined over the years. Both are rooted in an extremist jihadi ideology and are fiercely opposed to the presence of foreign troops in Muslim communities. They are interdependent militarily, financially, and politically. Yet important distinctions exist between the two. Al Qaeda is an Arab-based movement with a global agenda of attacking corrupt Arab regimes and the Western interests that support them. The Taliban is a complex, diverse network of Pashtun nationalists, dispossessed tribes, and Islamist extremists seeking to control the Pashtun-majority parts of Afghanistan and Pakistan. The insurgent coalition is "a fragmented series of shifting tactical alliances of convenience," according to Kilcullen, a network of extremist groups that are "loosely cooperating toward roughly similar objectives."[26]

Analyst Thomas Ruttig describes the Taliban as dualistic in nature. It consists of a vertical structure with a centralized shadow state and a leadership council still dominated by Mullah Omar and the movement's pre-2001 Kandahari power base. It also comprises horizontal, network-like structures rooted in segmented Pashtun tribal society, a "network of networks" in which religious, tribal, and regional interests overlap.[27]

Taliban groups do not have a transnational agenda. Unlike al Qaeda they have not committed aggression against or declared war on the United States. They are focused on removing foreign troops from their soil. In contrast to al Qaeda's global agenda, most Taliban factions focus primarily on local objectives and do not pose a direct threat to the United States.[28] The armed movements sometimes cooperate with one another but otherwise operate independently. Some have received funding and technical assistance from foreign groups, but very few share al Qaeda's agenda of waging war on the West.

While Taliban groups are motivated by local concerns, they share an increasingly significant pan-Islamist ideology. Their social and cultural roots are in distinct local tribal communities, but they claim to be supra-ethnic Islamists, who disregard tribal, ethnic, and linguistic differences and "only know Muslims." In their self-identification as Pashtuns or

Muslims, many Afghans have shifted toward the latter. Taliban activists consciously assert this supra-tribal Islamist identity as a way to keep the door open for non-Pashtun supporters. As Ruttig observes,

> This has allowed the Taliban to systematically expand into non-Pashtun areas of the North and West. "Islam" provides an umbrella that creates cohesion in an otherwise—ethnically as well as politically—heterogeneous movement.[29]

The Taliban's internationalist rhetoric has not translated into transnational action. Unlike the militants of al Qaeda, Pashtun fighters are not engaged in attacks beyond their homeland. No Afghans participate in al Qaeda's hierarchy, and no Arabs are in the Taliban's command structure. There is no recorded incident of an Afghan Talib participating in a terrorist attack outside the Af/Pak tribal region.[30]

Individuals like Times Square bomber Faisal Shahzad who attempt terrorist attacks in the United States are not seasoned fighters from al Qaeda or the Taliban. Many live in the United States or other Western countries, although born and with family connections abroad. They are not recruited in Afghanistan or Pakistan to attack the "far enemy" but are self-motivated to seek out the support and inspiration they need to carry out their criminal acts. They receive training, money, and material assistance, but they act on their own as individuals or in small groups. They are homegrown, to use the parlance of counterterrorism, motivated, as Shahzad stated in court, by anger and resentment at U.S. attacks on their homeland and interventions against Muslim countries.

Roots of Insurgency

The various Taliban elements are divided by ideology and purpose, but they are united by one overriding objective: to rid their region of foreign forces. They share a determination to resist American air strikes and military occupation. The recent increase in military operations and U.S.

troop levels has deepened this common commitment and generated greater armed resistance. Western military intervention has strengthened the Taliban and the local determination to resist.

The Taliban insurgency can be traced back to the anti-Soviet war of the 1980s and the rise of the mujahideen. As the United States sought ways to counter the Soviet invasion of Afghanistan, it encouraged the creation of Islamist militias. Washington poured more than $9 billion of mostly military aid into the mujahideen effort, most of it channeled through Pakistan. The Saudi government and other Arab states were encouraged to mobilize religiously motivated adherents of Islam to fight against the infidel communists. U.S. support helped to bolster some of the most brutal and abusive militia leaders in Afghanistan, including Gulbuddin Hekmatyar, who was brought to the White House in 1985 to meet President Ronald Reagan. One of those who participated in the mujahideen war was Osama bin Laden, who formed al Qaeda from veterans of the anti-Soviet jihad. As Middle East scholar Shibley Telhami observed, the policy of encouraging jihad "had unintended horrific consequences."[31]

The Taliban movement originated in and still draws much of its support from religious networks and *ulama*-led madrassas and mosques in Pashtun communities. The Taliban emerged as an organized movement in the early 1990s, according to Ruttig, "as a moral reaction against the atrocities and what it saw as a 'betrayal of Islam' by the post-Najibullah mujahideen regime of the so-called Islamic State of Afghanistan."[32] As the movement attracted support and began to show military prowess it was "adopted" by Pakistani military and intelligence officials, who supported and used the movement to advance Pakistan's national interests.

The violence and instability of contemporary Afghanistan are rooted in what Giustozzi terms the "crisis of Afghan rural society." The country is reeling from the combined shocks of thirty years of war, massive forced migration, a doubling of the population between 1978 and 2002, the loss of much agricultural land and livestock, and urbanization. The result is severe stress to the traditional tribal social order. The structures that previously held society together no longer provide stability, income, and social belonging. Youth lack a sense of purpose and are motivated to join extremist movements as an outlet for expressing frustration and gaining the prestige and sense of community no longer provided by the tribal system. External military attacks and incursions into the tribal areas exacerbate these tensions and further undermine the influence of elders and traditional figures of authority. As tribal elders lose influence, the clergy gain a more prominent political role and spread their radicalized view of militant jihad.[33]

Religious leaders tend to assume greater authority and political prominence during times of external threat. As they gain village leadership roles some mullahs urge men to grow beards and join the jihad. Surveys of clergy opinion find them hostile to the presence of foreign troops and unfriendly toward the Kabul government. Beginning as early as 2003 evidence began to emerge of a shift in the attitudes of the clergy toward supporting the insurgency. The Taliban draws significant support from these local conservative religious networks and the elements of the population under their influence. The disruptions caused by foreign intervention and insurgency have weakened traditional leadership structures and strengthened the role of conservative religious voices that advocate violent jihad.

Sources of Taliban Support

While opinion polls show that 90 percent or more of the Afghan people oppose the Taliban and do not want them to regain control of the country, the movement has a substantial base of public support or at least tolerance. In comparison to the corrupt rulers associated with the Kabul government, Taliban leaders have a reputation for honesty and efficient, if harsh, rule. By assuming the mantle of leadership in opposing the presence of foreign forces, they have won sufficient community support, or at least acquiescence, to grow into a formidable military and political presence, especially in the southern parts of the country. The claim that the Taliban is mostly a mercenary force, writes Giustozzi, "is at odds with strong evidence showing the commitment of Taliban fighters and their readiness to fight to the last man." Such allegations should be treated more as propaganda than assertions of objective fact.[34] The Taliban are mostly true believers, fiercely dedicated and willing to die for their cause.

As is true with any effective guerrilla force, the Taliban's survival depends on the consent of surrounding communities. Kilcullen explains that Taliban units are able to travel lightly and live off the land because "a measure of popular support exists for their agenda."[35] The Taliban method of fighting requires an ability to melt seamlessly into the local population. Insurgents could not withstand the superior firepower and technology of U.S. and NATO forces without the cover provided by surrounding communities. Intimidation no doubt plays a role, and Taliban militants have been ruthless in terrorizing those who betray them, but the insurgency has undeniable public appeal. A substantial part of the Pashtun population supports armed resistance against foreign forces and the Kabul regime.

In the areas they control the Taliban have set up their own form of administration, centered on the judiciary. They have imposed a rigid form of Sharia and reestablished draconian restrictions on women. Traditional informal judicial services are in high demand in the countryside because the Kabul government has failed to establish a reliable justice system. The Taliban's demonstrated ability to restore order, prosecute criminals, and dispense justice has been welcomed by those who are fed up with impunity and insecurity. The judicial system administered by the Taliban provides a greater degree of predictability and reliability than the arbitrary methods employed by government agents and security forces.[36]

Traditional informal justice systems predominate in the rural areas of Afghanistan. Najla Ayubi, a prominent Afghan lawyer and former member of the Independent Election Commission, estimates that 80 percent of conflicts in the countryside are addressed through traditional courts in which men make all the decisions and women have no formal role in the process.[37] These traditional courts, like those established by the Taliban, are highly discriminatory toward women. They reinforce legal practices and codes that deny women basic rights of property and judicial representation.

The anarchical situation in much of the country benefits the Taliban and helps to generate a steady flow of recruits. The Taliban draws its support from popular revulsion at the corruption and incompetence of local government and security forces. In many cases insurgents have been motivated to take up arms by the venality and brutality of the local leaders put in place by the Kabul government. Communities antagonized by the local authorities and security forces provide the largest number of recruits for the Taliban. "The insurgents did not have to do much," writes Giustozzi, "except approach the victims of the pro-Karzai strongmen and promise them protection and support." Police abuses include taking bribes as well as more malign actions such as extrajudicial executions, torture, and the arbitrary arrest of unarmed civilians in villages where the presence of Taliban fighters is suspected. Armed attacks by both Afghan and foreign troops have driven many people into refugee camps, which serve as recruiting grounds for the insurgents.[38]

A recent study by Matt Waldman for the United States Institute of Peace confirms that the Taliban insurgency is a reaction to perceived military aggression, foreign occupation, abuses of power, and political exclusion.[39] Waldman interviewed dozens of people in Kabul and Kandahar, including fourteen insurgents, and found that Taliban motivations are not unreasonable. They are fighting for what they consider just purposes. "While Taliban tactics may be abhorrent," Waldman writes, "many of their objectives could be considered valid." Their goals are congruent with the interests of much of Afghan society: the withdrawal of foreign forces and Sharia, which to most of those interviewed means a stronger emphasis on law and order. According to Waldman, if these objectives were met, most insurgents and their supporters would accept a negotiated solution.

A Flawed Partner

The daunting security challenges in Afghanistan are directly related to the governance failures of the Kabul regime. The success of counterinsurgency depends on a reliable and effective local government that is capable of rallying public support and providing an alternative to the insurgents. This essential ingredient is missing in Afghanistan. U.S. ambassador to Afghanistan Karl Eikenberry described the problem bluntly in his November 2009 cable to the White House:

> President Karzai is not an adequate strategic partner.... [He] continues to shun responsibility for any sovereign burden, whether defense, governance, or development.... Beyond Karzai himself, there is no political ruling class that provides an overarching national identity that transcends local affiliations and provides reliable partnership. Even if we could eradicate pervasive corruption, the country has few indigenous resources of revenue, few means to distribute services to its citizens, and most important, little to no political will or capacity to carry out basic tasks of governance.[40]

No counterinsurgency campaign can succeed without an effective political strategy for building representative and accountable governance. The most enduring lesson of previous COIN campaigns is the necessity for effective indigenous political leadership. The human capital of local civilian leadership is the decisive factor in creating so-called good governance. For governance to be good it must be responsive to public will. This means reducing corruption and abuse and empowering people to elect leaders who govern in the public interest. This is not something that foreign military forces can achieve, no matter how numerous and well trained they may be. No amount of military force can compensate for the absence of responsible governance.

The "essential strategic problem" for Western intervention in Afghanistan, writes Kilcullen, is "less about directly defeating the Taliban and more about building an Afghan state" that can solve the country's problems. For stabilization and reconstruction measures to have an effect, they must take place in the context of a comprehensive political solution, something that is "unlikely to occur in the foreseeable future."[41] According to the RAND study *War by Other Means*:

The greatest weakness in the struggle with Islamic insurgency is not U.S. firepower but the ineptitude and illegitimacy of the very regimes that are meant to be the alternative to religious tyranny— the ones tagged and targeted as Western puppets by jihad. Success thus hinges on improving the performance and accountability of governments in the Muslim world. This is the essence of classical counterinsurgency.[42]

The absence of representative governance is a principal source of violent extremism. Populations that are excluded from politics and estranged from authoritarian and corrupt governments are more likely to support insurgents committed to destroying such regimes. Marginalized communities often are a source of popular support for insurgents. If governments are unable or unwilling to provide safety and deliver public services, people will search elsewhere for the help they need.

The current regime in Kabul has never been and is unlikely ever to be capable of establishing effective governance over Afghanistan. Like the Saigon government during the Vietnam War era, the Kabul government is a foreign creation. The choice of Hamid Karzai as president and the creation of a centralized form of government were decisions taken by the United States and its allies at the international conference organized under UN auspices in Bonn in November 2001. The government was created through a top-down process without indigenous involvement and with little or no popular participation or support. From the very beginning the Karzai regime was based on an extremely narrow social base. Lakhdar Brahimi was the principal UN official in charge of the Bonn conference. In an interview several years later with former *New York Times* correspondent Barbara Crossette, Brahimi acknowledged that the people at that conference "were not fully representative of the rich variety of the Afghan people.... The popular base of the interim administration put together in Bonn under President Karzai was far too narrow."[43]

The initial weaknesses of the Kabul government were compounded by Karzai's decision to rely for support on former warlords and militia leaders. Of the first group of thirty-two provincial governors appointed in 2002, at least twenty were militia commanders, warlords, or strongmen. These appointed governors were able to place their followers in positions of leadership. This was especially the case in the important Ministry of Interior. The governance system created by Karzai was geared toward accommodating strongmen and warlords with their own power base and resources, not for appointing functionaries loyal to the central government to consolidate the influence of Kabul.[44] The United States encouraged Karzai in these decisions. Instead of relying on more legitimate networks of tribal and religious leaders and urban elites that had survived Taliban persecution, the United States and its allies bypassed these locally based actors in favor of discredited former leaders, many of them living abroad. As Theros and Kaldor write, "This top-down technocratic focus on state-building and reconstruction largely ignored local power dynamics and failed to meet the most critical needs of the population, creating the well-spring of disenfranchisement that fuels the insurgency."[45] Corruption and inefficiency have undermined government legitimacy. Afghan security forces are notoriously unreliable and have experienced large-scale desertions. In Kandahar, half the policemen trained by foreign forces walked off the job. Sometimes whole units have deserted. The Afghan National Army has also experienced widespread unauthorized absence and desertion. In some units in the southern part of the country absence and desertion rates have reached 50 percent. Some police units have been accused of collaborating with the Taliban and even of fighting against foreign troops. In the security forces, as in the general population, there is deep-rooted hostility toward the presence of foreign troops and a lack of confidence in the Kabul government.[46]

U.S. and British defense officials estimated in 2007 that up to half of all development assistance to Afghanistan failed to reach the people for whom it was intended. Kabul government officials siphon off much of that aid. Even when foreign assistance reaches local communities it tends to be hoarded by influential elders. Efforts to provide services to the population, such as digging deep wells, are often hijacked by local notables for their exclusive benefit.[47] The Afghanistan Study Group concludes that "Karzai government affiliates and appointees in rural Afghanistan have often proven to be more corrupt and ruthless than the Taliban."[48]

The Karzai regime has been and remains almost entirely dependent on foreign (mostly U.S.) assistance. In a country where few pay taxes, many have little cash income, and productive enterprises are lacking, the government has an extremely shallow financial foundation. The Kabul government on its own is not able to provide sufficient funds to the provinces to support economic development or to establish the authority and administrative reach of the central government. This weakness of state authority has been most acute in the south, where many districts are beyond its administrative and political control. The absence of effective state administration in many parts of the country has been a key factor in undermining the legitimacy of the Kabul government. Taliban forces have taken advantage of these weaknesses by targeting and causing the final collapse of whatever state administration may have existed. In many districts in Helmand, Uruzgan, and Zabul provinces, government administration has either disappeared altogether or is functionally nonexistent.

The United States and its partners have compounded the problem of poor governance by focusing their state-building activities on the creation of large-scale Afghan security forces. By far the greatest amount of governance-related foreign assistance to Afghanistan has been devoted to recruiting, training, and equipping the Afghan National Police and the Afghan National Army. This emphasis has been dictated by security concerns and is based on a militarized theory of development that seeks to build state capacity on the foundations of strong military forces. It is an approach that undermines civilian governance and drains resources from needed development programs. It is a formula for the further militarization of Afghanistan and the prolongation of armed conflict.

Development specialists have long known that high rates of military spending are detrimental to genuine economic development. The 1994 UN Human Development Report on "Human Security" found that high rates of military spending are associated with lower rates of economic development. The higher the ratio of military to nonmilitary government spending in a country, the lower the level of human development.[49]

The Kabul government has no capacity to pay for the massive security forces foreign governments are attempting to create. Actual government receipts (apart from massive U.S. military aid and the other forms of foreign assistance) are not sufficient to pay for existing force levels, let alone the additional expansion that U.S. leaders are planning. If proposals for further enlarging Afghan security forces are realized, Afghanistan will be saddled with an unsustainable long-term financial burden. It will become a foreign-dependent militia state for many years to come.

Military Stalemate

On paper the military balance in Afghanistan overwhelmingly favors the Kabul government and U.S./NATO forces. The Afghan National Army has grown to more than 130,000 and the Afghan National Police to approximately 100,000. U.S. forces number some 100,000; contributions from NATO and other countries and armed contractors amount to another 50,000 troops. The total for all forces aligned against the Taliban is thus more than 350,000. It is a force largely equipped with U.S. weapons technology, fortified by armor and artillery, and defended by the power of the U.S. Air Force, supplemented by both military and CIA drones.

Arrayed against this vast force is the ragtag insurgent force of the Taliban. According to Kilcullen, as of mid-2008 there were between 32,000 and 40,000 Taliban insurgents operating inside Afghanistan at any one time. Of these only 8,000 to 10,000 were full-time fighters or core Taliban. Several thousand part-time fighters operate in loose networks as part of a clandestine village underground, and a much larger sympathizer and supporter base exists in both Afghanistan and Pakistan.[50]

Despite being greatly outnumbered, Taliban insurgent forces have been able to gain momentum and strategic advantage in many parts of

Afghanistan. Giustozzi assessed the strategic situation in March 2007 as one of "stalemate, with a slight advantage for the Taliban."[51] Kilcullen and other military strategists have argued that it will require a concerted long-term effort lasting at least five to ten years to build a resilient Afghan state and civil society that can defeat the threat from a resurgent Taliban. The problem in Pakistan is even more complex and daunting.

Taliban leaders have a long-term strategy that seeks to wear down and outlast their more numerous and better-armed adversaries. They prioritize political goals over military objectives. Their strategy is not to defeat the opposing forces but to erode their political will and to demonstrate to local populations that they can resist and replace corrupt government authority. The insurgents are not able to challenge U.S. and NATO forces on the battlefield, but that is not really their aim. Conventional military victories are not relevant to their long-term strategy. The purpose of military action is to demonstrate through protracted armed struggle that the war is unwinnable for the government and foreign forces.

Taliban leaders have learned the lessons of guerrilla war, as practiced by Vietnamese, Algerian, and other insurgents in numerous campaigns over the decades. They avoid open warfare and instead focus on roadside bombings, suicide attacks, and intense but brief assaults that seek to harass and wear down U.S. and NATO forces. Their goal is to deny government forces and their foreign supporters control over the civilian population. One of the purposes of suicide bombing is to turn every civilian into a potential enemy in the eyes of government and foreign forces. This undermines security and stability and widens the gap between government and foreign troops on one side and Afghan civilians on the other. Preventing the government from controlling the population enables the Taliban to compete for popular loyalties and gain greater political influence.

Political countermeasures have worked alongside armed attacks to foil Western nation-building efforts. Foreign troops often find that villagers are unwilling to participate in Western-funded development projects. U.S. forces experienced this after entering the village of Marjah in Helmand Province in early 2010. Cash distributed by U.S. officers to local officials and villagers in some cases was turned over to the Taliban. The defiance and reluctance that U.S. forces often encounter among local populations result from fear of Taliban reprisals and genuine distrust and hostility toward the presence of foreigners.

What Is Success?

Continuing to occupy Afghanistan and wage a protracted counterinsurgency war against the Taliban is not necessary to achieve U.S. strategic objectives. General Sir Richards stated that attempting to achieve military victory over Islamic militants is unnecessary and in any case "would never be achieved."[52] If the goal is to prevent a Taliban takeover and preserve the framework of the current Afghan government, that objective already is being achieved. The Obama troop surge cannot bring military victory but it prevents the Taliban from taking power and increases the incentive for negotiating a political solution. Taliban forces dominate local districts, but they have not attempted and are not able to challenge the Karzai government directly in Kabul. Taliban fighters are able to inflict casualties on foreign and Afghan government forces, but they do not have the capacity to take over the government.

This is the view of writer and former British diplomat Rory Stewart, now a Tory backbencher in Parliament. Stewart doubts that U.S. and British forces can defeat the Taliban, and he questions why this is necessary. The brutality and primitive policies of the Taliban have alienated many Afghans. While the Taliban has some public support, few people in Afghanistan want to see a return to that bleak era, and conditions in the country have changed in ways that will prevent Taliban domination. The Hazara, Tajik, and Uzbek populations are more numerous in total than the Pashtuns who support the Taliban. The Tajiks and other ethnic groups are also more powerful militarily than they were when the Taliban took power in 1996. Most of the members of the Afghan security forces are Tajik. The non-Pashtun ethnic and political groupings in Afghanistan would "strongly resist any attempt by the Taliban to occupy their areas," Stewart writes.[53] Kilcullen agrees. If the ethnic groups that have been part of the Northern Alliance—Uzbeks, Tajiks, Hazaras—remain with the Kabul regime rather than forming separate military forces, they have the capability of preventing the Taliban from taking over the government.[54]

Afghan national security forces have been hapless in U.S.-led combat operations, but they might be effective in defending their own interests and defeating Taliban attempts to take over the Kabul government. The United States and allied forces would retain the option, even after military withdrawal, of stepping in with air support and precision bombing, as they did in 2001, to help local ground forces defeat a Taliban offensive against the government. The will and capacity of Afghan fighters to defend the Kabul government will depend more on political than military factors. If the regime becomes more transparent and less corrupt, and if the Taliban gain political representation and a greater share of power through national reconciliation, the likelihood of a war against Kabul diminishes, and the willingness of Afghans to defend their government increases.

The Fire Next Door

"The cancer is in Pakistan," President Obama told his aides during the fall 2009 White House strategy review.[55] It is an apt metaphor for describing the plight of a people and a nation struggling to contain the spread of militancy and violent extremism. Pakistan's role as a sanctuary and support base for the Taliban confers significant advantages to the insurgency, including a steady supply of recruits into Afghanistan. Pakistani influence is pervasive in southern Afghanistan, where most economic activity and trade are transacted in Pakistani rupees. U.S. military forces have fought for years without success to stem the flow of insurgents across the border. Giustozzi estimates that approximately 20 percent of insurgent casualties in Afghanistan are Pakistani, reflecting the approximate percentage of fighters who are of Pakistani origin.[56]

Most U.S. officials view Pakistan narrowly through the lens of the war in Afghanistan and the desire to eliminate terrorist safe havens and prevent the flow of Taliban recruits. For years Washington has pressured the Pakistani Army to take military action against insurgent groups in the Federally Administered Tribal Areas (FATA) and other districts along the border. The result has been greatly increased Pakistani military action (140,000 Pakistani Army and Frontier Scouts forces are deployed in the border region) but little progress in suppressing the insurgency or weakening a Taliban movement that Pakistan itself helped to create and has long supported.[57]

Pakistani officials are playing a double game. They apply pressure against some Taliban groups, particularly those that challenge their authority within the country, but they tolerate and sometimes support Taliban fighters doing battle with U.S.-led forces in Afghanistan. WikiLeaks documents confirm what many other sources have reported over the years: that elements of Pakistan's Inter-Services Intelligence agency provide support for the Taliban. According to intelligence documents reviewed by the U.S. General Accounting Office, al Qaeda and the Taliban have been active in Pakistan's FATA and border region since 2002, using the area as a base of military operations and spreading extremist ideologies.[58] The most recent White House report on Afghanistan and Pakistan notes that the Pakistani army continues "to avoid military engagements that would put it in direct conflict with Afghan Taliban or al Qaeda forces in North Waziristan. This is as much a political choice as it is a reflection of an under-resourced military."[59]

Faced with dissemblance and reluctance from its supposed ally, the United States has taken matters into its own hands, greatly increasing air strikes, drone attacks, and targeted assassinations in northern Pakistan. The number of drone strikes in Pakistan has increased significantly since Obama took office, as have the number of cross-border commando raids. More than twenty drone attacks took place in Pakistan in September 2010, double the rate of previous months.[60] U.S. commanders are launching as many as a dozen commando raids a night into the region.[61] In some cases U.S. combat helicopters have crossed the border, and on one occasion in October 2010 U.S. pilots killed Pakistani soldiers, touching off a major diplomatic incident between the two countries. Air strikes and drone attacks have killed dozens of militant leaders, but they have also caused a significant number of Pakistani civilian casualties, contributing to pervasive anti-Americanism throughout the country. High-tech weapons are able to hit targets precisely, but their effectiveness depends on accurate intelligence and a local population willing to share information. These are highly uncertain in the Pashtun tribal belt, where Taliban influence is widespread and growing stronger with the rising death toll from U.S. attacks.

Officials in Washington insist that Pakistani officials have given private approval for military attacks into their country, but Pakistani leaders have repeatedly condemned the attacks. During the dispute over the helicopter attack in October 2010, the Pakistani government declared that there is "no justification nor understanding" for U.S. drone strikes into their country. "We believe that they are counter-productive and also a violation of our sovereignty," stated Foreign Ministry spokesperson Abdul Basit.[62]

The fundamental problems in Pakistan are not military but political, social, and economic. Since its inception Pakistan has suffered from pervasive poverty, poor governance, glaring inequality, and widespread corruption. During most of its history Pakistan has been ruled by generals, and even when civilians are nominally in charge military leaders remain the power behind the throne. The country was born out of religious–nationalist separatism and has experienced profound traumas of war and ethnic division, exacerbated by decades of military competition with India. The two countries have fought three major wars and several skirmishes and for decades have been burdened by a debilitating arms race that has now gone nuclear and that diverts vast resources from the many millions in both countries who remain desperately poor.

The U.S. strategy of relying primarily on military solutions has failed in Pakistan as it has in Afghanistan. The risks of miscalculation are even greater in Pakistan, where in the event of state collapse violent extremists might get their hands on the bomb. Washington has recognized belatedly the need to address the fragile underpinnings of the Pakistani state and has provided greater assistance for economic and social development. The majority of U.S. funding continues to flow into Pakistani security programs, however, further militarizing an already over-militarized state. President Obama said that U.S. policy must aim to "excise the cancer in Pakistan." This is a necessary and worthy goal, but it will not be achieved through military means. Instead the United States needs to develop a long-term development strategy that focuses on bolstering civilian governance, human rights, and the rule of law, and that strengthens parliamentary, judicial, and law enforcement institutions that can stand up to military and extremist intimidation.

CHAPTER THREE

Gendered Intervention

WITH SARAH SMILES PERSINGER

S ince 2001 Afghan women and girls have taken great personal risk to renegotiate the strict gender roles and identities imposed upon them by tradition and the Taliban. With the support of the international community Afghan women have achieved social, economic, and political gains, although their overall condition remains difficult and in some respects has worsened. Since 2006, as insurgency and Taliban influence have spread, women have experienced renewed oppression in Taliban-controlled areas and diminishing political space and support within the Kabul government. They have suffered most in the area of security, as have all Afghans, victimized by widespread armed violence and deteriorating personal safety.

Reform and Reaction

Throughout Afghanistan's modern history, there have been fitful attempts by urban, ruling elites to advance the status of women. All have met with resistance and backlash from largely conservative, religious, and rural constituencies that have historically maintained a large degree of autonomy from the weak, centralized state. As in many Muslim countries, the question of women has been central to debates about the place of tradition, Islam, and modernity in state-building processes.[1] These previous attempts to reform women's status in Afghanistan reveal two predominant trends: resistance to state-led reforms from the tribal periphery and a tendency by political factions to exploit the issue of women. Because of the symbolic and cultural value of women in Islamic society, the issue of women's rights has often been used as a political tool by factions seeking to challenge the legitimacy of state power or buttress their claims to rule.

Afghanistan is a tableau of ethnic, religious, linguistic, and cultural diversity. Customs vary widely among Pashtuns, Hazaras, Tajiks, Uzbeks, Turkmen, and Aimaq communities, many of which have lived in isolation from one another against Afghanistan's mountainous terrain. Generalizations about women's status or static cultural mores are unhelpful. While some Pashtuns in the southern belt of Afghanistan adhere to an observance of *purdah,* or gender segregation, Pashtuns elsewhere are considered less conservative. The Hazaras have historically been more liberal toward women.[2] While class, ethnic, tribal, kinship, and religious affiliations have determined individual agency and opportunities for women, state-building processes, geopolitical conflicts, and the impact of war on Afghan society over the past several decades have been equally decisive in shaping women's futures.

Over the decades the status of women in Afghan society has fluctuated in response to changing political conditions. During the Soviet-dominated era in the late 1970s, the number of women serving in government, working in jobs, and attending school increased, although deeply rooted gender stereotypes and violence against women continued behind closed doors. During the following decade, dominated by the mujahideen war against the Soviets, women were marginalized and were largely barred from public life. Conditions worsened during the civil war of the early 1990s and the period of Taliban rule. After the overthrow of the Taliban, significant changes were adopted in the law to provide greater public opportunities for women, and social conditions began to improve. With the growth of insurgency and the deterioration of security conditions, some of the recent improvements in women's rights have eroded.

Mujahideen and Taliban

Following the collapse of the Soviet Union and withdrawal of Soviet troops from Afghanistan in 1989, the client regime of President Mohammad Najibullah hung on to power until 1992. Mujahideen commanders took control of large parts of the country and started fighting among themselves. The country was engulfed in a devastating civil war. Already flimsy state institutions were destroyed. An estimated 1.5 million Afghans were killed and 7 million displaced. Gross human rights abuses ensued, with women raped, mutilated, trafficked, forced into prostitution, and pressured to marry commanders. The number of widow-headed households increased, and refugees poured into Pakistan and other neighboring countries. Women were sequestered in refugee camps, where some were empowered through educational opportunities offered by aid groups.

State failure paved the way for the emergence of the Taliban, whose leaders, such as Mullah Omar, hailed from the most rural, underdeveloped, and conservative Pashtun provinces in southern Afghanistan. Upon taking power, the Taliban enforced a strict interpretation of Sharia law and Pashtun customary law, or *Pashtunwali,* which was anathema to many other ethnic groups. Men were forced to grow beards, and women were dismissed from their jobs and banned from working outside the home. Girls' schools were closed and women were forced to wear the *chaddori* (veil) or *burqa.* Marauding zealots from the Department of the Promotion of Virtue and Prevention of Vice set about smashing TV sets and banning all forms of entertainment. The Taliban's Religious Police were particularly vicious toward women. Bizarre edicts were issued banning women from wearing makeup, wearing white socks, or even hitting the floor with their shoes when they walked. More insidious edicts banned women from going to the hospital or leaving their homes without a male family member or *mahram*. In 1998, all houses were ordered to blacken their windows so women could not be visible from the outside.

Women, viewed as powerful symbols of Islamic virtue and honor, were used as vehicles by the Taliban to coercively control the wider society. Taught by their mullahs that women were a temptation, Talibs sought to subjugate women to show their zeal as true believers. Ahmed Rashid argues that the suppression of women was a fundamental marker that differentiated the Taliban from the former mujahideen. Punishing women was also seen as a mark of manhood and used to keep morale high among Taliban fighters. After military defeats, the Taliban tightened strictures on women. As international censure of such practices grew, the regime increased the severity of punishments with public executions, amputations, and stoning of women.[3] While women secretly resisted the Taliban's policies by running home schools and finding novel ways around Taliban rules such as hiring *mahrams* to leave the house,[4] the Taliban's policies had a devastating impact on their lives and a society already beleaguered from years of war.

Improving Women's Rights

These torments ended when the Taliban regime was driven from power in 2001. In subsequent years Western states and donor agencies poured billions of dollars into programs to improve the condition of women and guarantee their political rights. These efforts brought significant improvement in the lives of women, as follows:

- The availability of health care improved dramatically. Across the country clinics and hospitals have been constructed or rebuilt and more health workers have been trained. Access to health services has increased from virtually no coverage in 2001 to more than 80 percent coverage today. Immunization rates have increased, and infant and child mortality rates have declined.[5] With support from international organizations, the Ministry of Public Health (MPH) has developed and introduced obstetric care in many districts and has launched information campaigns on hygiene and maternal care.[6]

- The availability of trained midwives and birth attendants has grown significantly. During the Taliban era midwifery schools were shut down, and few trained attendants and health professionals were available. After 2001 the MPH reopened many midwife centers, and in 2005 it established a national Midwifery Education Accreditation Board.[7] The number of trained birth attendants in 2010 was estimated at 2,400, five times more than during the Taliban years.[8] The percentage of births attended by skilled care remains low but increased from 14 percent in 2003 to 19 percent in 2007.[9]

- Progress has been achieved in providing economic opportunities for women, primarily through community development grants in the National Solidarity Program (NSP) and microcredit access. A quarter of the participants in democratically elected NSP councils are women, who are able to benefit from local grant programs. Small-scale microcredit programs have multiplied, providing more than 1.5 million loans in recent years. The majority of loan recipients are women. Community grants and microcredit programs provide opportunities to earn a living outside the home. They also improve women's sense of worth and well-being.

- Greater access to primary and secondary education has been a major priority of the Afghan government and international donors. Enrollment numbers have increased significantly, with more than seven million schoolchildren enrolled in 2010. This is a more than sevenfold increase over school attendance rates during the years of Taliban rule.[10] Girls could not attend school during the Taliban era but now compose 37 percent of the student population.[11]

- Since 2001 Afghan women have gained significant political rights. The Taliban completely excluded women from political participation, but in recent years women have begun to re-enter political life. The Afghan Constitution approved in 2004 establishes a quota of 25 percent of seats in parliament for women. Since 2001 women have been free to vote and participate in elections, with women comprising approximately 44 percent of voters in the 2005 parliamentary election.[12]

- In August 2009, President Karzai signed a law on the Elimination of Violence against Women (EVAW). This was a significant landmark that creates a legal basis for gender equality and establishes standards for both public and private spheres of behavior related to marriage, physical abuse, and access to education and other social opportunities.

The substantial efforts by governments, international agencies, and civil society groups to protect and enhance the rights of Afghan women are laudable. The United States, the United Nations, and European governments in particular deserve credit for prioritizing civilian development efforts to improve the health of women and girls and advance their economic, social, and political rights. The gains for women's rights are important and need to be preserved in any future negotiated peace agreement. Social and economic programs that have been successful in advancing women's rights and life opportunities should be continued and expanded into the future.

Insecurity, Public and Private

Progress in advancing women's rights has been precarious, however, and is jeopardized by setbacks in security and personal safety. The rising tide of violent conflict in Afghanistan has created increased hardships and suffering for both women and men. The U.S.-led military intervention has expanded but has not been able to guarantee security. After improving with the overthrow of the Taliban, security conditions worsened after 2006. Women have been victimized not only by violence between foreign forces and insurgents, but also by opportunistic criminal gangs and predatory local government officials and police chiefs.

In Afghanistan as in all wars, women have suffered the special torment of sexual violence. Armies and militias through the ages have used the power of the gun to force their will upon women. Patterns of sexual exploitation and violence have been repeated in recent decades through Afghanistan's ordeal of civil war, foreign intervention, and insurgency. During the 1980s Afghan women were sexually assaulted by both Soviet soldiers and mujahideen fighters.[13] According to Soraya Parlika, head of the National Union of Women of Afghanistan, "under mujahideen regime, the weapon of one community against the other was to attack, to jail, to rape, to hit in public the female members of the other community."[14] The civil war period of 1992 to 1995 witnessed a significant increase in abuses against women, according to research by Amnesty International. Women were abducted, raped, forced into prostitution, and coerced into becoming "wives" to militia commanders. Rape was used as a weapon of war, with sexual assaults meant to dishonor a woman's entire community.[15] The UN Special Rapporteur reported in 2000 that the number of sexual assaults increased significantly in Kabul during the civil war.[16] Rape, sexual abuse, and gender-based violence increased all over Afghanistan.[17]

These abuses continued during the Taliban regime. Prostitution and trafficking of women increased, especially among refugees.[18] One reason for this, according to international aid workers, was the imposition of Taliban restrictions on women's access to education and work. Lacking the possibility of earning a living and feeding their children, many women were forced to turn to prostitution or became victims of trafficking.[19] During the brief war to overthrow the Taliban in the fall of 2001 both Taliban combatants and fighters of the United Front/ Northern Alliance engaged in sexual violence and rape against women.[20] The 2002 report of the UN secretary-general on discrimination against women and girls in Afghanistan found an "increase in the number of abductions of young girls and women by Taliban fighters."[21]

The pattern of sexually related violence against women has continued into the current period of insurgency and counterinsurgency. Several studies indicate that sexual exploitation and the trafficking of women have risen since 2001. Human Rights Watch reported in 2003 that Afghan government soldiers and commanders were raping girls, boys, and women in provinces in the south and east.[22] In 2009 the group reported that cases of rape and forced prostitution of children had risen. A study by the International Organization for Migration (IOM) in 2008 focused on problems of increased trafficking and sexual exploitation resulting from rising insecurity, population displacement, poverty, and traditional social practices and beliefs.[23] Women for Women International reported in 2009 that 43.9 percent of women believe that incidents of rape have increased since the fall of the Taliban, while 32.2 percent believe there has been an increase in forced prostitution.[24]

Women face various forms of indirect violence, in public life and in the home. Violence against women is measured not only in the number of deaths and injuries but also in the number of lives stunted, in the experience of women who spend their lives confined to the home, unable to leave without a *mahram*. It is measured in the lives of women who have no say in deciding which husband to marry, who are unable to read or write, and who have no employment or opportunity to accumulate wealth and property. Conditions of indirect violence in Afghanistan are rooted in a persistent lack of economic development and the denial of access to education, health care, and other essential assets required for a life of security and fulfillment. These conditions have been exacerbated by decades of war and violence and most recently by the intensifying conflict between insurgents and counterinsurgents.

A common but little-acknowledged form of indirect violence is the practice of arranged marriage. Girls are often forced to marry at an early age and in arrangements decided by parents and relatives. It is a practice that has existed for centuries and is considered acceptable by many— although its effects can be very harmful and may leave severe social and psychological scars on the affected children and their families. UNICEF research in 2001 indicated that 54 percent of girls and 9 percent of boys in Afghanistan are married before the age of eighteen.[25]

The custom of early marriage is rooted in economic and social conditions. Families sometimes seek to improve their social position or increase their wealth by marrying their daughters to men of influence and means.[26]

In the tribal code of the Pashtuns, marrying off a daughter is a way for the family to atone for an offense or pay a debt. Such practices are considered by many rural Afghanis means of maintaining "justice" and social harmony—although by international standards they are a form of slavery.

Evidence suggests that early marriages become more frequent during times of war and insecurity. This may reflect the desire of parents and family members to have their daughters married safely to preferred husbands rather than victimized by rape or forced into marriages with militia or Taliban fighters. In neighboring Tajikistan during the 1992 civil war, the number of early marriages rose sharply when fighting erupted, later declining when the war ended.[27] UNICEF staff professionals in Kabul believe that a similar pattern exists in Afghanistan today as "civil war and militarization have led to an increased number of forced marriages of young girls."[28]

Forced marriage is a crime under the Afghanistan Penal Code, but child marriage is not. Civil law gives fathers the right to arrange marriages for daughters who are fifteen years or older. The laws are rarely applied, however, and in practice many girls younger than fifteen enter into arranged marriages.[29] Research published in 2005 by the Max Planck Institute found that child marriages are much more frequent in rural communities than urban areas.[30] Most women outside the cities are married before the age of eighteen. The WCLRF study also revealed a correlation between literacy rates and child marriages. Most parents who force girls to marry are illiterate (71 percent).

Domestic violence is widespread in Afghanistan, where women are often perceived as the personal property of their husbands.[31] Women suffer from physical abuse and various forms of subjugation and humiliation by family members. The full extent of the problem is unknown, since domestic violence is rarely reported. A woman making such charges may suffer further abuse or even death and could bring shame and hardship on her family. The Afghan Independent Human Rights Commission has been documenting cases of violence against women since 2001 and has reported an increased number of cases, although this could be due to improved reporting prompted by TV and radio announcements encouraging women to provide information. International donors have supported the establishment of shelters for abused and vulnerable Afghan women. These shelters offer safe haven for women fleeing domestic violence and sexual abuse. They provide support that is otherwise unavailable to abused women. Conservative members of parliament and the police have attempted to close the shelters, spreading rumors that women in shelters are prostitutes.

Life and Health

After the overthrow of the Taliban, Afghanistan's health system was in a state of "near-total disrepair."[32] Decades of war had devastated health infrastructure and left the numbers of health care professionals extremely low, notably among female doctors, nurses, and midwives—the latter due to the Taliban's ban on female education and closure of midwifery schools.[33] Today conditions are better, but life expectancy remains one of the lowest in the world, approximately 45.5 years, compared to 68 in neighboring Pakistan, 72.5 in Iran and the worldwide average of 68.9.[34] Survival rates have steadily improved, as they have throughout the world, but progress has been interrupted by wars, insurgency, and political repression. The rate of improvement slowed during the period of anti-Soviet war in the 1980s and leveled off completely during the civil war and years of Taliban rule in the 1990s. Life expectancy figures remained flat in the initial years after 2001 but more recently have improved.

In most countries women live on average three or four years longer than men. In Afghanistan, however, there is virtually no difference between male and female life expectancies. Afghan men and women have had virtually identical life expectancies for decades with never more than a few months separating them. This demographic anomaly reflects the severe stresses of life in this harsh land, including social and cultural factors that affect women acutely.

The maternal mortality rate in Afghanistan is estimated at 1,600 deaths per 100,000 live births, the second worst in the world next to

Sierra Leone, with the risk increasing in remote areas.[35] Fertility rates are also very high, on average 6.6 children per mother, which increases the risk of maternal death.[36] Most of these maternal deaths are preventable. High maternal mortality rates result from inadequate access to health care, poor sanitary conditions, the absence of family planning services, and pregnancies that occur at a young age.

High maternal mortality rates partly explain why life expectancy for women in Afghanistan is so low. Because women bear so many children, often in conditions of inadequate health care and without a trained birth attendant, they are at much greater risk of death. Complications arising from pregnancy and childbirth are exacerbated by the high rate of child marriage. Young teens giving birth before their bodies are fully developed are more likely to experience life-threatening pregnancy complications.

Infant and child mortality rates in Afghanistan are also among the world's worst. In an environment of insecurity, acute poverty, malnutrition, and poor sanitation, nearly one in five Afghan children dies before his or her fifth birthday, according to World Health Organization (WHO) data. Infant mortality rates are declining in Afghanistan, as they are globally, but the number of preventable infant deaths remains shockingly high.[37] The rate of infant mortality declined from 165 per 1,000 live births in 2001 to 129 per 1,000 in 2006, according to the *Bulletin of the World Health Organization*.[38] All studies find a sharp urban-rural disparity, with mortality rates much higher in rural areas.

The absence of midwifery services and skilled health workers during delivery are major causes of high maternal and infant mortality rates. A UNICEF study for the years 2001–2003 estimated that health care professionals attended to fewer than 14 percent of deliveries. The rate was much higher in urban areas, 34.8 percent, compared to only 6.9 percent in rural areas.[39] In recent years, the percentage of births attended by health workers has increased, and the availability of trained attendants has grown, with the number of trained graduates of midwifery schools now estimated at 2,400.[40] This increase is the result of a major effort by the Afghan government and international donors to provide trained midwives. The urban/rural disparity persists, with most of these midwives located in Kabul and other cities and few trained health workers available in rural areas.[41] Nonetheless the overall improvement in the availability of maternal care is considerable.

Efforts to improve health care generally have been substantial. Across the country clinics and hospitals have been constructed or rebuilt and more health workers have been trained. Immunization rates against diphtheria, pertussis, and tetanus have increased from 54 percent of infants in 2003 to 85 percent in 2008.[42] With support from international organizations the MPH has also developed and introduced obstetric care in twenty districts, and has launched information campaigns on hygiene and maternal care.[43] The National Action Plan for the Women in Afghanistan (NAPWA) strives to improve the availability of health care and medical services, especially in rural areas. It promotes the reduction of maternal mortality, improved access to family planning, and greater women's representation in the heath sector.[44]

The main sources of financial support for these improvements in health care have been external. Donor contributions exceed Afghan government spending on health by a ratio of more than nine to one, with foreign assistance to Afghanistan's health sector standing at just over US$223 million for 2008, according to government figures. The three main donors are the World Bank, the United States Agency for International Development (USAID), and the European Commission.[45] It is critically important that assistance for improved health care in Afghanistan continue and increase in the years ahead. Support for increased access to maternal care should be sustained as new political alignments and power-sharing arrangements unfold. Hopefully all political factions can agree on the value of efforts to save Afghan women and babies from tragic, needless deaths.

Economic Opportunity

During the Taliban era women were not allowed to work or engage in economic activity outside the home. As a result, the number of female beggars increased.[46] Since 2001, women have gained employment opportunities, although they still face many obstacles to entering the workforce. Women are still considered responsible for family life and are expected to cook and clean for their husbands, children, and extended family members upon returning from work. Some women face family disapproval for working outside the home. Women thus have to struggle on two fronts—in the workplace and at home—to assert their right to earn an independent income and participate in economic activity.

Despite the obstacles, real progress has been achieved since 2001 in providing economic opportunities for women. Two of the most significant vehicles for female economic empowerment are the NSP and microcredit support for small-scale enterprise. The NSP has evolved as an effective program for decentralized, locally based economic development. A recent article in *Foreign Affairs* described it as "the most widely hailed development program in Afghanistan."[47] Under the NSP program the Kabul government provides grants to democratically elected community councils for local projects. The NSP includes approximately 22,300 Community Development Councils (CDCs) in 361 districts. According to recent figures, 24 percent of the participants in CDCs are women.[48] The CDCs have initiated more than 51,000 projects involving water and sanitation, rural roads, electrification, irrigation, and human capital development.[49]

The NSP program is important as a means of enhancing women's economic and social rights. A significant portion of its funding is dedicated to women. A World Bank evaluation found that the NSP makes a positive contribution to increased women's participation in economic and community life. According to the study, "NSP stimulates the provision of dispute mediation and greater engagement of women in community activities. The program also appears to make men more accepting of female participation in the selection of the village headman and increases the prominence of, and respect for, senior women in the village."[50]

Women's access to microcredit is developing rapidly in Afghanistan. Microfinance institutions are the principal source of credit for many Afghanis, with twelve times more clients than all commercial banks combined. The Microfinance Investment Facility of Afghanistan has fifteen implementing partners, which serve 434,095 savings and loan clients. It has 306 branches in 26 provinces across Afghanistan. It has distributed a total of 1.5 million loans worth more than $751 million.[51] The number of female clients is substantial. BRAC-Afghanistan (an affiliate of the Bangladesh Rural Advancement Committee, the world's largest development agency) has 86 percent female clients, while the OXUS-Afghanistan Development Network has 48 percent female clients.[52] USAID-funded microfinance projects have 128,000 clients in Afghanistan, 75 percent of them women. Microcredit loans have been used for bee-keeping, poultry farming, kitchen gardens, home-based dairy production, and handicraft production.[53] Because of the lack of security in the country, microfinance institutions mainly operate in the central, western, and northern provinces, limiting the access to microcredit in the south and east.[54]

Microcredit programs not only provide women with the opportunity to earn a living outside the home but also improve the well-being and sense of self-worth of women participants. A recent survey of microfinance programs found 99.3 percent of women participants reporting increased self-confidence. More than 98 percent reported feeling more respected in society.[55] More than 95 percent reported increased mobility both inside and outside their residential area.

Local economic-development programs have achieved progress, but they have limitations. Many women receiving support through these programs are confined to traditional female crafts such as sewing at home. Few work in male-dominated fields such as retail sales. In some families, men manage the money earned by women.[56] The long-term effects of community development and microfinancing projects are also mitigated by the fact that most are drafted from an emergency short-term relief framework rather than with long-term development in mind.[57] As a result, the long-term sustainability of these programs is uncertain.

Education and Literacy

Afghanistan is one of the least educated countries in the world. According to the Human Development Index it is ranked 181 out of 182 countries in literacy, trailed only by Niger.[58] The literacy rate for women is especially low. According to the UN Development Fund for Women (UNIFEM), the literacy rate for women is 16 percent, compared to 31 percent for men.[59] The World Bank estimates female literacy at 21 percent.[60]

Formal literacy programs did not begin in Afghanistan until 1969. By the 1990s literacy rates began to climb toward 30 percent for men, but women lagged far behind at only 7 percent. During the period of Taliban rule, women and girls were not permitted to attend schools—although informal teaching continued in secret, and some mullahs used mosques as classrooms for girls.[61] After 2001, literacy classes resumed, sponsored by the Afghan government, international organizations, and Afghan nongovernmental organizations (NGOs). Most of these programs have been concentrated in cities and towns, with less educational availability in rural provinces.

A lack of security has negatively affected access to education in many parts of the country, retarding progress toward higher literacy rates. The 2009 study "Knowledge on Fire," sponsored by CARE, showed that southeastern Pashtun majority areas with high rates of violence have lower literacy rates for men and women, while western and northern regions fare better. In the eastern province of Khost near the Pakistan border, the literacy rate for females is just 7 percent, compared to 44 percent for men. In Logar province near Kabul, literacy for women is 9 percent, compared to 21 percent for men. In the largely Tajik province of Balk in the north, literacy for women is 21 percent, and it's 53 percent for men. Multiple factors account for the wide variation in literacy rates among provinces and regions. The ethnic composition and cultural traditions of the population, geographical location, and the security situation all influence rates of literacy and access to education.

Since 2001 improving access to primary school has been a major priority of international donors and the Afghan government. Evidence shows that educating girls produces myriad private and public benefits: they marry later and have fewer and healthier babies and lower maternal mortality rates. Girls' education also boosts women's participation in the labor force, which is greatly needed in Afghanistan. Significant improvements have been registered in enrollment numbers, the training of teachers and the rehabilitation and construction of school buildings. According to recent UNESCO data:

- There are 7.3 million students enrolled in primary and secondary schools—37 percent female—compared to fewer than 900,000 students (all male) in 2002.
- There are 12,000 schools in Afghanistan, 4,480 of them established since 2002.
- Teacher numbers grew from 20,700 (all men) in 2002 to 158,000 in 2008—28.8 percent female.
- More than 61 million textbooks for primary and secondary schools are being distributed.
- Thousands of students are enrolled in community-based schools, which provide education to children in areas without government school facilities.[62]
- There are 62,000 Afghans enrolled in universities.[63]

While primary education has increased significantly, attendance rates in secondary school are very low for both boys and girls, with high attrition rates.[64] Gender disparities persist. Boys are almost three times as likely as girls to reach secondary school and four times as likely to graduate.

As insurgency has intensified in Afghanistan in recent years, schools and female students have become frequent targets of violent attack. Hundreds of schools have been burned or destroyed. Girls' schools have been the primary target. According to the CARE study, 40 percent of the attacks on education in 2006 were against girls' schools, although they represented only 19 percent of all schools. Thirty-two percent of attacks in 2006 were on combined schools, and the remaining 28 percent of attacks were on boys' schools. Attacks against schools countrywide increased dramatically, jumping from 241 in 2006 to 670 in 2008.[65]

During 2009, some 200 poison attacks took place against students in Afghanistan. Almost all of these attacks were against female students.[66]

More than 650 schools were closed that year because of insecurity, depriving more than 340,000 children, including girls, of the right to education.[67] In April 2010 more than one hundred girls and women teachers fell ill in Kunduz province, although initial forensic tests did not confirm poisoning as the cause. In May 2010, seventeen girls fell ill at Durkhani High School in Kabul and were taken to hospital. A spokesman for the Ministry of Education, Asef Nang, told reporters that "there are destructive elements who don't want girls to continue their education."[68] As security risks increased, informal home-based literacy centers spread, hidden from public view, much like during the Taliban years.

Taliban leaders claim that they are not opposed to education as such but rather to mixed male-female classes and the attendance of non-veiled girls. They oppose new curricula introduced in recent years and object to what they claim is the propagandist role of teachers against the mujahideen. The Taliban did not object to the reopening of a school in Musa Qala in Helmand Province once the British troops had been withdrawn. In January 2007 the Taliban announced that they would open their own schools in the areas under their control, initially only for boys and later for girls too.[69] Such claims are not credible given the continuing violence against schools and the record of Taliban opposition to education in the past. The Taliban concept of learning is limited to segregated instruction in religious fundamentalism. This in no way qualifies as proper education and does not confer literacy and scientific knowledge.

The CARE study examined eight provinces to try to understand the nature of recent attacks against educational institutions and programs. The study found that resistance toward girls' education is not universal in Afghanistan and greatly depends on factors like ethnicity, religion, and geography. The interplay of these factors has resulted in differing views on education among the groups and regions within the country. A mistrust of educational institutions and foreign influence fuels much of the cultural resistance to schooling in general and to girls' schools in particular.[70]

Although many schools in Afghanistan have been targeted with violence, most have escaped attack and continue to operate, even in areas affected by insurgency. The pattern of violence against schools suggests a clear differentiation between those that are built and managed locally and those that are established by the Kabul government or international agencies. CARE, the Afghan Institute of Learning, and BRAC-Afghanistan run hundreds of locally controlled schools that have not been attacked by insurgents. Schools that have strong community ties survive. Those that are imposed from the outside, either by Kabul or international organizations, are more likely to be burned.

The successes of Greg Mortenson and his Central Asia Institute are based on a formula of local involvement and community control. As of 2010 the Institute had established 131 schools in rural areas of Afghanistan and Pakistan, with a focus on improving female literacy. Only one of these schools has been attacked. "Aid can be done anywhere, including where the Taliban are," according to Mortenson. "But it's imperative the elders are consulted, and that the development staff is all local, and no foreigners."[71]

Strong local support exists for education and the defense of schools in many Afghan communities. This is evidenced, according to Antonio Giustozzi, by the "widespread formation of self-defense units among villagers to protect state schools." These self-defense units have been formed at nearly half of Afghanistan's 9,000 educational institutions.[72] Schools that are indigenously based have community support and are able to survive. This is the formula for providing greater educational opportunity for Afghan girls and boys.

Political Representation

Since 2001 Afghan women have won greater rights to participate in political decision-making. These rights have been precarious, however, more *de jure* than *de facto*, and recently have eroded under pressure from both the resurgent Taliban and conservative male leaders in the Afghan government. During the years of Taliban rule women were excluded from political participation, reversing the minimal gains achieved in the reforms of the 1970s and 1980s. After the fall of the Taliban, women began to re-enter political life and gained new legal rights. Article 22 of the 2004 Constitution ensures gender equality: "The citizens of Afghanistan—whether woman or man—have equal rights and duties before the law." This achievement is tempered, however, by the language of Article 3, which states that "No law can be contrary to the beliefs and provisions of the sacred religion of Islam." This vague wording has been used to justify the imposition of Sharia and its discriminatory application toward women.[73]

One of the most significant achievements in the Constitution is the quota reserving 25 percent of the seats in parliament for women. This is an impressive achievement for women in any country. The lower house of the Afghan parliament, the *Wolesi Jirga,* has a higher rate of female participation than most of the world's legislatures, including the Congress of the United States. In addition, nearly 17 percent of seats in the *Meshrano Jirga,* the upper house, are reserved for women. The quotas provide for at least two women from every province.

It is uncertain, however, whether these female members of parliament (MPs) have actual decision-making power and whether their voices are heard and respected by the men who continue to make the major political decisions. The constitutional gains are widely viewed to have increased the "presence, not the power" of Afghan women.[74] Many Afghan women parliamentarians are aligned with warlords and vote according to their sectarian and factional interests, rather than as a cohesive bloc. Only a limited number of women have served in cabinet posts, and those selected have been chosen according to their political connections, not on merit.

Because of rising insecurity and the spreading atmosphere of intimidation and impunity, female participation in government has decreased. Women in leadership positions have faced intimidation and even death threats and in some instances have been forced to leave public office. A number of outspoken public women have been murdered and attacked. Women's participation in the civil service of Afghanistan decreased from 31 percent in 2006 to 21.4 percent in 2009. There are no women in the

Supreme Court and very few serve as judges (4.2 percent), police officers (0.4 percent) or soldiers in the army (0.6 percent). President Karzai
initially appointed women to head three cabinet departments, but today
only one remains, the Minister of Women's Affairs.[75]

The Ministry of Women's Affairs (MWA) of Afghanistan was
established by the Karzai government with strong international encouragement following the Bonn Conference. Advocates for women's rights
had urged that gender mainstreaming be established across all ministries
rather than concentrated within one department, but that advice was
ignored. Instead the Karzai government followed the established pattern from previous Afghan governments in the Soviet era by creating
a special department for women's affairs. Other government ministries
assign gender focal points to cooperate with the Ministry of Women's
Affairs, but most of the appointed people are low-level officials with
little or no decision-making authority.[76] The MWA has never enjoyed
real power or influence and has faced constant criticism and attack
from reactionary forces. Dr. Simla Samar was appointed the first head
of the new ministry and was named a deputy prime minister, but she
was forced to resign from her position after just six months due to death
threats against her.[77]

The MWA sponsors programs of vocational training, concentrating
on traditional skills such as sewing, carpet weaving, flower making, and
interior decoration. These training classes help to meet women's short-
term needs, but over the long run they reinforce narrow gender roles and
offer little opportunity for women to develop politically and economically.
The Ministry also supports literacy programs and has gradually developed a broader range of initiatives, including the prevention of violence
against women, but it has limited resources and relies substantially on
international assistance. Women who serve in the Ministry complain that
they are sidelined in government decision-making. In general, the MWA
has done little to advance women's political and economic power.

With the support and encouragement of international agencies, the
Afghan government has adopted NAPWA, a ten-year plan to improve
the status of women. Drafted with the help of UNIFEM and launched in

March 2008, the ambitious plan sets out gender mainstreaming bench-marks in the realms of security, human rights, political participation, economic opportunity, health, and education.[78] The plan has helped in mobilizing international donors to support specific programs for women, but it has had little impact in practice. Implementation of the plan rests with male-dominated Afghan government institutions, which now and in the past have shown little interest in advancing women's rights.

The right to vote was granted to women in Afghanistan in 1964, although this right existed more on paper than in reality and did not give women political autonomy. An Asia Foundation survey prior to the 2004 elections found 87 percent of respondents (both women and men) agreeing that women need their husbands' permission to vote, with 72 percent agreeing they should seek the advice of male relatives on which candidates to support.[79] Women in Afghanistan have made progress in political participation since 2001, but female candidates and voters continue to face harassment and threats of violence against themselves and their supporters.[80] Even when women are able to vote they are not always free to make their own choices, and they face pressure to follow the instructions of their husbands or other male family members.

Despite these obstacles, many women have stepped forward to par-ticipate in elections. They have been encouraged to vote by educational programs and support from the international community. The high point of female participation was the 2005 parliamentary election, in which women comprised approximately 44 percent of voters.[81] As insurgency and Taliban influence spread, however, women's electoral involvement declined. In the August 2009 voting for president and provincial coun-cils, female participation decreased. The officially reported rate of female electoral participation was 38 percent, but the actual turnout was much lower, as intimidation and threats turned away many would-be voters.[82] A gender advisor at the Independent Election Commission in Kabul esti-mated that the female voter turnout in 2009 was less than 20 percent.[83]

The September 2010 parliamentary elections were marked by widespread corruption and the intimidation of candidates—especially women.[84] The Free and Fair Foundation of Afghanistan reported that the Taliban sent night letters to candidates warning them not to run, including threats of violence to female candidates in Logar province south of Kabul.[85] More than 900 polling stations across the country were closed because of the violence.[86] The Electoral Complaints Commission in Afghanistan received thousands of complaints before and during the election of ballot stuffing, intimidation, and fraud.

Many women have run as candidates for elected office. In 2005 344 women were among the 2,835 people registered as parliamentary candidates.[87] The number of women candidates increased to 413 for the 2010 elections, despite rising threats and violence.[88]

Political Reversals

The political rights of women have come under increasing pressure in recent years, the result of two interrelated developments—the resurgence and spreading influence of the Taliban and the resistance of reactionary political factions within the Kabul government. The Taliban-led resistance to foreign intervention in Afghanistan has been based in part on a misguided desire to save Afghan women from the presumed contamination of Western modernity. Many of the political leaders who serve in the Kabul government and the *Wolesi Jirga* have similar beliefs and are viscerally opposed to the empowerment of women. The warlords and militia commanders upon whom the Karzai regime depends have become increasingly brazen in seeking to undermine the political rights of women. These male leaders resent attempts by Western governments and local activists to empower women.

Words such as "gender" and "gender mainstreaming" have no equivalent in *Dari* and are seen by many as Western constructs that are alien to Afghan society. A study of three government ministries by the Afghanistan Research and Evaluation Unit (AREU) showed confusion about the meaning of the term *gender*—many interviewees believed it to be synonymous with women—and criticism of the concept as both foreign and un-Islamic.[89] The AREU study proposed a number of mechanisms for promoting gender equality, including training and stronger government mandates, but all such proposals run up against the Kabul government's demonstrated lack of political will for enhancing the rights of women.

In February 2009 the Afghan parliament approved the Shia Personal Status Law. Ironically President Karzai signed the measure on the same day he signed the EVAW law.[90] The Personal Status Law was introduced prior to the 2009 presidential election and was part of Karzai's effort to hold onto office by pandering to conservative Shia factions. The law regulates the lives of Shia Muslims in the areas of marriage, divorce, and inheritance. Among other controversial provisions, the law stipulates that wives must submit to sexual intercourse with their husbands every fourth night—the legalization of marital rape. The law prevents women from leaving their homes without permission from their husbands, and grants custody rights to fathers and grandfathers in the event of marital separation. Under pressure from international actors, President Karzai agreed to have the law reviewed, but only minor amendments were eventually made.

When the Afghan electoral commission exposed pervasive fraud in the 2009 election, President Karzai responded by abolishing the commission. In February 2010 he issued a presidential law creating a new electoral body that diminished the independence of this supposedly independent watchdog agency. The *New York Times* described this as a "travesty" that is "hugely destructive" to the integrity of a U.S. mission in Afghanistan, which is supposedly intended to foster good governance and democracy.[91] The new law also contained provisions that attempted to limit the number of women in parliament. The interpretation of the law is in dispute, but an international official quoted by the *Washington Post* expressed concern that it could "substantially reduce" the number of women in parliament.[92] The law also established more onerous requirements for political candidates, tripling the required fee to 30,000 Afghans, the equivalent of $600. This poses special burdens on women, who generally lack independent income and are financially dependent on men. Candidates must also produce 1,000 signed election cards to qualify for office. Again this poses special obstacles for women, who are less able to campaign house-to-house for signatures because of deteriorating security conditions. The electoral law was rejected by parliament, but constitutional ambiguities have left the matter in dispute.[93] Regardless of the legal status of the presidential decree, it clearly reflects the intention of Karzai and his cronies to usurp power and restrict the political rights of women.

A July 2010 Human Rights Watch report describes an Afghan parliament dominated by ideologically conservative political factions, including Hezb-i-Islami.

> Parliament has often displayed hostility towards women's rights, issuing repeated calls for the Ministry of Women's Affairs to be dissolved and casting aspersions on safe houses for women and girls. In 2008 a parliamentary committee drafted a bill that would introduce Taliban-style prohibitions, such as bans on women and men talking in the street and on shops selling revealing clothing. In late 2009, after the enactment of the Shia Personal Status Law, conservative factions in Parliament attempted to weaken the Elimination of Violence Against Women (EVAW) law by revoking articles criminalizing child marriage and domestic violence, which were deemed to be in contradiction with Sharia.[94]

It is important to note that these reactionary tendencies have emerged within an Afghan government that depends entirely on the support of the United States and other foreign governments, and in the presence of some 140,000 foreign troops supposedly sent to uphold democracy and freedom. By continuing to fund and protect such a regime, Washington and its allies have become complicit in actions that are contrary to their stated intentions.

Of course the alternative to the Karzai regime could be worse. A Taliban takeover of government would eliminate the few political gains that have been achieved. Many Afghan women are concerned that political reconciliation with Taliban leaders would make the government even more reactionary and lead to the further erosion of women's rights. This is a very real danger, but it is also likely that further restrictions on women's political rights will continue under the present government. Even with an increased number of troops on the ground and vast sums provided for economic assistance, the United States and its partners have found themselves with little leverage over the shape of Afghanistan's internal politics. This is a sobering reminder of the limits of foreign intervention and the inability of even the most powerful states to guarantee through external pressure democracy and human rights in another country.

CHAPTER FOUR

Development and Security

International leaders and policy experts have long recognized that
overcoming terrorism requires a holistic strategy that addresses the
underlying conditions that give rise to violent extremism. In 2004 UN
secretary-general Kofi Annan cautioned that security-oriented measures
alone are not sufficient to overcome the global terrorist danger. The report
of his High-level Panel on Threats, Challenges, and Change called for
a comprehensive approach that balances security with development, the
rule of law, and the defense of human rights.[1] In his March 2005 report,
"In Larger Freedom," Annan emphasized the need for an integrated approach: "development, security, and human rights go hand in hand....
We will not enjoy development without security, we will not enjoy security without development, and we will not enjoy either without respect for
human rights. Unless all these causes are advanced, none will succeed."[2]

In 2006 the UN General Assembly adopted a *Global Counter-Terrorism Strategy* that embodied Annan's call for a more comprehensive and
integrated approach. The strategy transcends a narrow security-oriented
focus and links the struggle against terrorism to a broader set of principles
for avoiding violent conflict through development, democracy, and diplomacy. It identifies four pillars of international policy, the first of which is
addressing "conditions conducive to the spread of terrorism." It defines
"conditions conducive" as "prolonged unresolved conflicts; dehumaniza-
tion of victims of terrorism in all its forms and manifestations; lack of

rule of law and violations of human rights; ethnic, national, and religious discrimination; political exclusion; socio-economic marginalization; and lack of good governance." The primary way to fight terrorism, according to the strategy, is to adopt preventive measures such as resolving conflict, ending foreign occupation, overcoming oppression, eradicating poverty, advancing human rights, and promoting sustainable economic development and good governance.[3]

Securitized Aid

In principle, U.S. leaders endorse this holistic counterterrorism strategy and recognize that military approaches alone will not succeed in Afghanistan and Pakistan. When the Obama administration began its military buildup in 2009 it also announced a "civilian surge." The stated purpose was to enhance economic development and democracy building as means of ameliorating the conditions that give rise to terrorism. This implied a commitment to addressing the root causes of violent extremism.

In practice, however, U.S. operations in Afghanistan and Iraq are dominated by the Pentagon. Programs for development and democratization are subordinated to military priorities. The increases in civilian programs announced by the Obama administration have been dwarfed by the enormous commitment of additional resources for military operations. A few hundred civilians have been deployed to Afghanistan to assist with governance and economic development programs, but more than 50,000 additional troops have been sent to the region. The United States has increased its spending for military operations from approximately $2 billion a month in 2008 to more than $7 billion a month. The proposed civilian effort pales by comparison.

Many purported civilian aid programs are being channeled through the Pentagon and integrated into military operations. Only a small part of overall U.S. funding (an average of $1.5 billion a year since 2001) actually goes toward humanitarian and development needs, and much of that never actually reaches the Afghan people. An estimated 25 percent of reconstruction funding goes for security forces to protect aid workers. On top of that are extensive administrative costs for agency managers and for various subcontractors of U.S. government-funded projects.[4] In the end, many of the acute humanitarian and development needs of the Afghan people go unmet.

To date much of the U.S. funding for development in Afghanistan has been channeled through Provincial Reconstruction Teams (PRTs), which are dominated by the military. The PRTs have been widely criticized for militarizing the provision of development aid and erasing the distinction between military and humanitarian activities. A subcommittee of the House Armed Services Committee in the U.S. Congress reported that PRTs tend to pursue "short-term, feel-good projects (with success measured by money spent or satisfaction of the local governor) without consideration of larger strategic and capacity-building implications."[5] Although they are intended to support reconstruction, the PRTs often have the effect of impeding development. By assuming some of the responsibilities that Afghan institutions should be fulfilling, the PRTs displace local capacity and weaken government accountability to its citizens. Many Afghans are afraid to work with the PRTs for fear of insurgent attacks directed against these foreign-run institutions. This makes it difficult for impoverished Afghan people to receive urgently needed assistance.

A report from the Center for Global Development criticized the PRTs as being "overwhelmingly military in scope and operation." Their primary focus is force protection and security assistance, not development. The PRTs have suffered from "generally poor development practice" and "relative lack of attention to promoting good governance and the rule of law." Problems identified with the PRTs include "inadequate civilian resources and personnel, no baseline assessments, meager strategic planning, and few metrics for assessing the impact of activities."[6] A January 2010 report by seven humanitarian agencies in Afghanistan argued that PRTs often lack the capacity to manage effective development initiatives. They are unable to gain the trust of local populations and thus cannot foster the sense of community ownership and local empowerment that are needed to achieve sustainable development. In many cases, PRTs rely on wasteful and corrupt contractors with limited capacities and weak links to local communities.

Related to the PRTs is the Commander's Emergency Response Program (CERP), which gives U.S. military commanders the authority to make direct cash payments to local contacts. The CERP program operates with little or no monitoring and evaluation. No centralized system exists for tracking how CERP money is spent or assessing the impact of the payments, which makes it impossible to know if they are contributing to development. The CERP budget for 2010 was more than $1 billion.[7] This approach is more likely to create dependency than self-sufficiency in local communities. It does not bring about genuine economic development, and its security benefits are short-term at best.

Money as a Weapons System

The development aid that is provided in Afghanistan is not for the purpose of alleviating poverty and supporting long-term sustainability. Its strategic objective is to gain the sympathy of local populations and win political support for the Afghan government against insurgent forces. Aid programs from the United States and other NATO countries generally flow to regions and communities where intensive combat operations are taking place. Aid programs serve military rather than humanitarian and development purposes. David Kilcullen notes: "in a counterinsurgency environment it is much less effective to apply governance and development assistance on a purely needs-based or universal basis. This soaks up resources with minimal political effect, and does little to counter the accidental guerrilla phenomenon."[8]

U.S. military leaders are explicit in describing development assistance as a tool of security policy. A recent U.S. Army manual for Iraq and Afghanistan was titled "A Commander's Guide to Money as a Weapons System." The document defines aid as "a nonlethal weapon" that is utilized to "win the hearts and minds of the indigenous population to facilitate defeating the insurgents."[9] This policy of subordinating traditional goals of mitigating poverty to a counterinsurgency military agenda blurs the analytic boundaries between security and development while politicizing both and detracting from efforts to improve the lives of disadvantaged communities.

The 2010 report by humanitarian agencies in Afghanistan summarized the dire consequences of this approach:

> More and more assistance is being channeled through military actors to "win hearts and minds" while efforts to address the underlying causes of poverty and repair the destruction wrought by three decades of conflict and disorder are being sidelined. Development projects implemented with military money or through military dominated structures aim to achieve fast results but are often poorly executed, inappropriate, and do not have sufficient community involvement to make them sustainable. There is little evidence this approach is generating stability and, in some cases, military involvement in development activities is, paradoxically, putting Afghan lives further at risk as these projects quickly become targeted by antigovernment elements.[10]

The channeling of development assistance to areas affected by violence leaves many needy and vulnerable populations without help. Funding is concentrated in southern provinces where insurgency and counterinsurgency are most prevalent, while other less turbulent parts of the country—in the north, center, and west—receive fewer development resources. This disparity creates inequalities, fuels resentment in the neglected areas, and provides additional fodder for Taliban recruiters as they expand their reach beyond the south.

Undermining Aid

Development programs are traditionally the province of civilian agencies, not military services. U.S. armed forces are not designed, trained, or equipped for nation building and social stabilization purposes. Their primary area of competence is the application of destructive force. They are not specialists in economic development, judicial reform, and the creation of accountable governance structures. Assigning such tasks to soldiers rather than civilians displaces the role of civil society and undermines the principles of local self-reliance and grassroots empowerment that are vital to genuine development and democratic governance. The work of development and democracy building must be performed by civilians, especially local people, through the active engagement of public officials and civil society. Security protections are needed for the civilians who carry out these tasks, and U.S. and NATO troops can help to bolster local forces in this mission, but external military involvement cannot accomplish the core tasks of assuring development and effective governance.

The practice of subordinating humanitarian and development assistance to military purposes is a violation of the Code of Conduct of the International Committee of the Red Cross. The Code provides for a strict separation of humanitarian assistance from any military or political agenda and emphasizes that support should be provided solely on the basis of human need.[11] This separation is necessary to safeguard aid workers as well as the communities they serve. Aid projects that are linked to the military mission in Afghanistan violate this principle. They generate mistrust within rural communities and sometimes provoke armed resistance.

The increasing level of military involvement in civilian development programs has undermined the independence and impartiality that are necessary for effective humanitarian action. Aid agencies under these circumstances are not impartial actors but are often perceived as partisans taking sides in a political military dispute.[12] Partly as a result, aid workers and their supporters have been targeted more frequently by insurgents as accomplices of Western interference and military occupation.[13] This was the tragic fate of members of the International Assistance Mission, when ten civilian medical workers, including some who had worked in the country for decades, were murdered in Badakhshan in August

2010. Dozens of aid workers have been killed in Afghanistan because of their perceived connections to military occupation and repressive government policies.

Violence against aid missions has become a global problem. The bombings of UN offices in Baghdad in August 2003 and Algiers in December 2007 were tragic manifestations of this phenomenon. The UN report following the Algiers bombing noted that "in many places the UN is no longer seen as impartial and neutral," but rather as serving a Western agenda. Humanitarian missions have been "negatively affected" by their association with "international and national military forces, security arrangements that do not seek acceptance from local communities" and the perceived "subordination of humanitarian activities to partisan political considerations." In such circumstances, said the report, the UN is seen as being "on the wrong side of justice."[14] Militarized aid programs are corrupting the integrity of humanitarian assistance and economic development activity. The growing resistance to these programs endangers aid workers, domestic and international, and the communities they serve.

The Agency Coordinating Body for Afghan Relief (ACBAR), a coalition of ninety nongovernmental humanitarian aid organizations in Afghanistan, issued a statement in 2002 that the "military should take the necessary steps to ensure that communities, policymakers, and the general public do not confuse military- and civilian-implemented assistance.... At no time should the military refer to its engagement in assistance as 'humanitarianism' or to NGOs as 'force multipliers' as both misnomers blur the distinction between civilian and military led interventions."[15]

The Limitations of Development

In counterinsurgency theory, civilian development and governance programs are intended to serve a political strategy of "separating the insurgent from the people and connecting the people to the government."

The goal is to win local allies, build local governance capacity, and bring tribes that had supported the insurgency onto the government's side. The Petraeus doctrine advocates combining military action with concerted efforts to win hearts and minds through rapid provision of humanitarian and economic assistance. Combat operations are to be accompanied by targeted development assistance and permanent population security measures.

Some localized successes have been achieved by such efforts. Kilcullen describes an effort in Kunar province to partner with local communities in separating Taliban insurgents from the people. This was accomplished by bringing tangible benefits of governance and development to the population and helping local people choose their own leaders through elections. The program focused on a road-building project, which served as a catalyst for broader social and political development. The greatest benefit was not the road itself, although it provided real improvements in transportation and commerce, but rather the process of engaging the local community in the planning and building of the road. The project provided jobs and alternative ways to improve the community. It helped to involve people in public decision-making and established a connection between the local community and government. These activities, U.S. officials hoped, would dissuade people from joining and helping the Taliban.[16]

Development projects such as the Kunar project do not stand on their own, however. They require large-scale external assistance and security protection from outside forces. Development projects of this type depend on permanent-presence protective security forces that remain in the affected locality on a sustained basis. This approach requires a large number of troops. The problem for counterinsurgency, however, is that the presence of external military forces may spark a rejection response and lead to armed resistance, undermining the very security that is necessary for development. It is a vicious cycle from which escape is not possible as long as military occupation persists. Kilcullen acknowledges that the Kunar model is not sustainable on a long-term basis. It is merely an example of a method for "stabilizing key areas on a temporary basis."[17]

Development and aid depend on reliable security. A pure development approach is not possible in opposed environments. Historical studies have shown that in civil wars and insurgencies, popular support tends to accrue to locally powerful actors rather than to those who can provide patronage benefits. This is the concept of the "strongest tribe," used by military analyst Bing West. The more organized, locally present, and militarily dominant a group, the more likely it will be able to enforce its will. This puts the onus of counterinsurgency back onto the military. Ultimately the intervening force must attempt to establish control over the affected community and deny insurgents the ability to operate. If this is not done, all the development and humanitarian assistance in the world will be of little use. Yet the attempt to impose security through external military intervention generates insurgency and undermines the security that is necessary for development.

The counterinsurgency approach to development is based on an unfounded and naïve assumption that development assistance will generate gratitude and encourage affected communities to cooperate with external forces. If local populations receive development aid, the theory goes, they will be more likely to back the local government and sever connections with the insurgents. Field experience in both Afghanistan and Iraq has shown, however, that insurgent mobilization and intimidation easily overcome any residual gratitude that may be generated by the building of roads or schools. In many instances the local response is not gratitude but resentment and armed resistance.

The potential benefit of economic development is undermined by the corruption and structural contradictions that are endemic to Western aid policies. Afghans interviewed by Marika Theros and Mary Kaldor recounted many stories of poor quality control in infrastructure-development projects, particularly in road construction. Interviewees told of subcontractors taking commissions off the top "before using the last remaining dollar to lay the thinnest layer of asphalt, resulting in roads that crumbled within months." Many complained that schools built through international developmental assistance lack basic structural integrity, making them unsafe for students and teachers.[18]

Aid projects in Afghanistan, as in other developing countries, are plagued by multiple tiers of subcontractors and poor oversight. Thousands of international contractors and technical assistance specialists have descended upon the country, often implementing programs with little or no local input. Aid programs tend to be supply driven and reflect donor preferences rather than the real needs of the population. Afghans see large numbers of foreigners employed at jobs in their country while they remain without work. A 2008 report from Matt Waldman found that 40 percent of all international aid funds intended for Afghanistan is spent in donor countries to pay consultant salaries and contractor operations.[19] These and other dilemmas of conventional development programming further erode the effectiveness and credibility of aid as a tool of Western policy.

Development for Security

Development can help to reduce the likelihood of civil conflict, but only if it is sustained over a long period and generates broadly based and substantial improvement in economic and social well-being. The link between development assistance and the prevention of armed extremism is well established in social science research and international practice. Studies by Paul Collier, Monty Marshall, and many others have demonstrated that a lack of economic development is the single greatest factor associated with the outbreak of civil war. Programs that enhance economic development are an effective means of reducing armed violence and preventing war.

In 2003 the Development Assistance Committee of the Organisation for Economic Co-operation and Development issued the paper "A Development Co-operation Lens on Terrorism Prevention." It traces terrorist insurgency to the frustration and anger that arise from social exclusion and political injustice, conditions that effective development policies can help to address. "Donors can reduce support for terrorism by working towards preventing the conditions that give rise to violent conflict," the report argues, especially among disaffected groups.[20] Many governments subsequently used this report as a justification for diverting some of their development assistance funding toward security-oriented programs, with a focus on security-sector reform and training.

The policy of funding security activities through overseas development budgets has aroused opposition among development groups and civil society actors. Many development and humanitarian professionals are alarmed at what they see as the redirection of aid away from poverty reduction and social development toward a counterterrorism and security agenda that serves the interests of states in the Global North rather than the needs of marginalized people in the South. Development advocates have sought to shield aid programs from military encroachments, even as they recognize the deep and inexorable connections that exist between development and security.

Accepting the need for a more integrated and coherent approach to development and security does not justify "the slow bleeding of financing for development purposes into security-related military activities," declared a report for CIDSE, the coalition of Catholic development agencies in Europe and North America.[21] Nor does it mean that all development and security goals are compatible. APRODEV, the Association of World Council of Churches Related Development Organisations in Europe, acknowledged that development can contribute to security, but only if the integrity and autonomy of development activities are respected fully. Faith-based agencies emphasize their commitment to the preferential option for the poor and the powerless and to the vision of a more just and peaceful world. They support a holistic human security strategy that prioritizes the well-being of individuals and communities rather than a narrow approach that protects the interests of states. They argue that human rights and development should be seen as ends in themselves, not as means to other purposes. Development cooperation should not be subsumed to an idea of security based on defending the interests and preserving the way of life of states in the Global North. Peace cannot be imposed from above. To be sustainable, peace must grow from below.[22]

The hearts-and-minds dimensions of counterinsurgency in Afghanistan have been no more successful than the military components. Despite considerable international effort to provide economic assistance and improve governance, little progress has been achieved. Development and democratization efforts have remained subservient to military operations. Aid programs have foundered on intractable problems of insecurity, corruption, and the rejection of foreign intervention. The report of humanitarian agencies in Afghanistan concludes, "The militarized aid approach is not working for Afghans, and more of the same is unlikely to yield different results." The prioritization of military needs over genuine development and good government has come at a high price, in human terms and in failed security policy. Poverty, unemployment, and weak, corrupt governments are known drivers of armed conflict. They must be ameliorated to achieve lasting peace.[23]

The aid agencies have proposed the following agenda for addressing these dilemmas and prioritizing development in a new, less militarized strategy for Afghanistan:

- Provide greater support for successful programs in public health, community-based development, and education.
- Phase out PRTs and other forms of militarized aid and increase capacity and funding for national and international civilian aid programs.
- Provide equitable delivery of humanitarian and development aid throughout the country in line with national development plans.
- Ensure improved capacity, responsiveness, and transparency of local government.
- Secure a greater role for the UN in delivering and coordinating aid.

CHAPTER FIVE

Security Solutions

Less-militarized means are available for meeting the legitimate goals of countering al Qaeda and preventing global terrorist attacks. The alternative to the strategy of continuous war is the pursuit of carefully calibrated military disengagement as a means of winning political concessions and reducing support for armed insurgency.[1] This is the approach recommended in the 2009 Carnegie Endowment report. U.S.-led forces should halt offensive military operations and focus on protecting civilians. A demilitarization strategy would reverse the logic of current U.S. policy, using the presence of foreign troops not in pursuit of illusory victory over Taliban insurgency but as a bargaining chip to induce political agreement and reconciliation.

Many worry that the Taliban will take over when foreign troops leave, but there is little chance of this, and it will be even less likely if sound strategies are followed. The natural balance of political and military power in Afghanistan favors the more numerous Tajiks and other Northern Alliance groups over the Pashtun-based Taliban. The Northern Alliance groups control the government and Afghan security forces and would resist any Taliban attempt to take power in Kabul. The Obama troop surge has tipped the balance further against the insurgents and increases the incentive for seeking a negotiated solution. If a power-sharing agreement can be negotiated that satisfies some of the Taliban's political ambitions, this would diminish the motivation for further insurgency. The United States can exert leverage over the Taliban by beginning the withdrawal of its military forces and by conditioning further withdrawals on security and political cooperation. U.S. and allied military disengagement should be linked to concrete Taliban steps toward security cooperation against al Qaeda and political power sharing and reconciliation at home. An interim protection force could be deployed to facilitate the withdrawal of foreign troops and provide security guarantees. A diplomatic compact among neighboring states would promote military neutralization and regional stabilization to prevent a Taliban takeover. All of these elements could combine to contain Taliban influence and create conditions for improved security in the absence of foreign troops.

The Logic of Disengagement

The strategy of demilitarization to enhance security seems paradoxical. How can we improve security by reducing the number of troops? The logic of this unorthodox approach stems from an opposite paradox—that foreign military intervention has undermined security. U.S./NATO leaders assume that greater military pressure will eventually subdue the Taliban and reduce the level of violence, but the trends so far have been in the opposite direction. The increasing involvement of U.S. and allied troops has been a principal cause of insurgency and the growth of Taliban influence. The alternative strategy attempts to reverse this dynamic. It seeks to remove the causes of the insurgency through a withdrawal of U.S. and other foreign troops. It attempts to weaken the Taliban by preempting its primary purposes and reducing its recruitment appeal.

The alternative approach sets paradox against paradox. It wagers that removing the causes of insurgency can reverse the deadly logic of escalating violence. It places the proposal to cease offensive operations and begin troop withdrawals within a comprehensive strategy that prioritizes political, diplomatic, economic, and social initiatives that seek to engage key local stakeholders. Gradual military demobilization would

be linked to a broader set of security conditions that emphasize cooperation against al Qaeda and opposition to the use of Afghan territory for
terrorist operations. It would be tied to a political process of reconciliation and power-sharing with the Taliban. It also would be combined
with increased support for locally based economic development and a
continuing commitment to political, economic, and social policies that
enhance human rights and the health and well-being of women.

A comprehensive package of interlocking arrangements, listed below,
will be needed to enhance security and stability.

- A reconciliation and power sharing agreement between the Kabul
  government and the Taliban within the framework of the current
  constitution
- A formal security agreement between the United States and a
  broadened Afghan government, linking troop withdrawals to a
  mutual cease-fire and cooperation in suppressing al Qaeda
- A social compact between international donors and the Afghan
  government to uphold constitutionally mandated rights and programs for social and economic development
- A properly resourced and actively supported UN-sponsored diplomatic contact group among neighboring states to secure and
  stabilize Afghanistan

The essential first steps are to cease combat operations and begin
troop withdrawals. President Obama should proceed with his stated
intention to start the military drawdown in July 2011, sooner if possible.
The initial reductions could be modest and would proceed according
to a flexible timeline that gives the United States leverage over related
political, security, economic, and social developments. The commitment
to leave completely and the timetable for doing so would be used to
leverage Taliban compliance with security cooperation agreements and
the acceptance of constitutional provisions. The withdrawal process and
the external financing that sustains the Karzai regime would provide
leverage to foster political reconciliation and human rights.

The political and social elements of the comprehensive package will require intensive negotiations and political bargaining—within Afghanistan, between Afghan authorities and the United States, between the Kabul government and international donors, and among neighboring states. As chief supporter of the Taliban, the Pakistani military will need to be involved in these negotiations. The United States must exert leadership in all of these efforts, but the negotiations and resulting agreements should be placed under UN auspices wherever appropriate. Troop withdrawals would be used to spur the negotiation process and would depend on fulfillment of the resulting security and sociopolitical agreements. Military disengagement would be combined with a greatly increased commitment to development, diplomacy, and the protection of human rights.

A Security Agreement

Military disengagement should be linked to the negotiation of an Afghanistan security agreement, similar to the security agreement reached with the Iraq government in 2008. The proposed agreement would seek to reduce armed violence, achieve mutual de-escalation, and establish conditions for longer-term security and stability in the region. The agreement would be negotiated with the Kabul government, under UN auspices, but the process would need to include parallel talks with Taliban leaders to ensure that all armed actors are committed to the plan. The parallel talks with the Taliban could be part of a broader process of negotiated reconciliation and power sharing. In return for a role in government and the withdrawal of foreign forces, the Taliban would be required to cooperate in suppressing al Qaeda and preventing the use of Afghan territory for terrorist activity. Internal security arrangements would be linked to a UN diplomatic initiative among neighboring states to contain Taliban influence and prevent external military interference.

Some officials of the Karzai government will be reluctant to share power with the Taliban and will resist an agreement for U.S. withdrawal. They like being propped up by U.S. troops and are happy to continue receiving billions of dollars in financial assistance—while engaging in corrupt practices that subvert democracy and undermine security and human rights. Washington needs to send an unambiguous message to Kabul that the days of free riding are over and that continued international support will depend on a new set of security and political conditions.

The security plan would include provisions for cease-fire and a halt to combat operations and armed attacks on both sides. For the U.S.-led coalition this would mean ending military patrols, commando raids, and bombing attacks, including drone strikes. U.S. and international troops would retain the right to defend themselves if attacked but would not go on the offensive. They would continue to train Afghan security forces, but their primary mission until they leave would be civilian protection. Massive construction projects for new air bases would be halted and Washington would begin to close or turn over its existing military bases.

The United States can calibrate the processes of military disengagement and increased financial support for the Kabul government to exert leverage on both the Taliban and the Karzai administration. The pace of withdrawal could be slowed or accelerated depending on whether the parties defy or cooperate with political, security, and social commitments. If the Taliban continue their attacks and renege on security and political cooperation, the pace of withdrawal could be slowed. Political and financial support for the Kabul government could be ramped up or down in response to its readiness to share power with the Taliban and accept agreed-on conditions for protecting women's rights.

With a cease-fire and the beginning of military withdrawals, the number of civilians killed and injured by armed violence will decline. The end of U.S. combat operations and bombing raids would immediately reduce the casualties caused by allied forces. It would also reduce the number of casualties resulting from insurgent attacks, which would become less frequent with allied forces off the roads and no longer besieging neighborhoods. The many deaths now caused by indiscriminate insurgent bombs and suicide attacks would diminish. Internecine political violence would probably continue, but this hopefully could be tempered by political power-sharing agreements. The frequent insurgent attacks against Afghan security forces would diminish if Taliban representatives were part of the government that commands these forces and if former insurgent fighters were integrated into the forces.

An Alternative Protection Force

The proposed security agreement could include an interim peacekeeping force to replace Western troops and provide transitional security protection. The Afghanistan Study Group proposes an international peacekeeping force for the country but provides no details for how this might be created or structured. Taliban representatives have suggested the deployment of an international Muslim-led protection force, and they have pledged not to attack such a force. The proposed security force could operate under the auspices of the UN, with a mission of providing population-centric protection during an interim period.

The deployment of an interim Muslim-led security force would help to facilitate the withdrawal of foreign troops and bolster Afghan security. It might increase the willingness of the Taliban to accept security and political cooperation agreements. It could provide security protection for women and others who might be threatened by insurgents and warlords as foreign forces withdraw. The required interim security force would not need to be large, once allied military operations cease and insurgent attacks diminish. A modest force of perhaps 30,000 troops might be sufficient. It would need to be paid, trained, and equipped by the United States and its NATO allies. As U.S.-led forces cease operations and pull back to their bases in advance of withdrawal, the interim security force could be introduced. Remaining foreign troops could assist with training and equipping the force. The UN Security Council could be asked to authorize the security agreement and the interim security force, which would operate for a limited period with the consent of the Afghan government under UN authority.

Of course no such interim security force exists, and creating it would require an enormous effort by the United States. The U.S. Army has well-established security training and education programs with the armed forces of Indonesia, Egypt, Saudi Arabia, Jordan, and other Muslim states. The armed forces of Bangladesh have had extensive experience serving in UN peacekeeping operations. U.S. diplomats and military commanders would need to meet with counterparts in these countries to seek troop contributions and establish an appropriate independent command structure. The United States and its NATO partners would leave behind sufficient equipment, including helicopters and vehicles, to enable it to operate.

A Comprehensive Strategy—Constraining Taliban Insurgency and Improving Security

Action	Outcome
Foreign military disengagement	Dampens the motivation to fight and reduces the appeal of insurgency
Political reconciliation and power sharing within Afghanistan	Gives the Taliban partial responsibility and integrates some insurgents into national security forces
Diplomatic contact group of neighboring states	Promotes military neutralization and noninterference by neighboring states
Interim protection force	Maintains security and provides civilian protection as foreign forces depart
Sustained large-scale support for development and human rights	Preserves the gains of women and funds programs that address conditions conducive to violent extremism

A "Grand Bargain"

Peacemaking and diplomacy are essential elements of an alternative security strategy. South Asia experts Barnett Rubin and Ahmed Rashid have proposed a political and diplomatic initiative with the Taliban that would isolate and peel away support from al Qaeda–related extremist groups. The Rubin-Rashid plan calls for luring "reconcilable" elements into political accommodation arrangements. They propose a "grand bargain" that would "seek a political solution with as much of the Afghan and Pakistani insurgencies as possible, offering political inclusion, the integration of Pakistan's indirectly ruled Federally Administered Tribal Areas (FATA) into the mainstream political and administrative institutions of Pakistan, and an end to hostile action by international troops in return for cooperation against al Qaeda."[2] Rubin and Rashid note that local Taliban representatives have expressed interest in such a bargain, in return for the withdrawal of foreign troops. The peace jirga of June 2010 in Kabul endorsed a variation of this approach as a political means of ending the war. Widespread support for a negotiated solution exists within the Afghan population. A February 2009 opinion poll in Afghanistan found 64 percent of respondents supporting a policy of negotiating with the Taliban and allowing its members to hold public office if they agree to stop fighting.[3]

Taliban sources have stated repeatedly that the departure of foreign troops from Afghanistan must be part of any negotiated settlement for ending armed hostilities. They have also demanded an end to U.S. drone attacks and the removal of Taliban names from the blacklist of terrorist suspects maintained by the UN Security Council. Although Taliban representatives are unequivocal in demanding the withdrawal of foreign forces, they have indicated flexibility in negotiating the terms of such an agreement.[4] Previously Taliban leaders demanded foreign withdrawal as a precondition for negotiation, but more recently they have agreed to enter into preliminary discussions with Kabul about political reconciliation without demanding the prior removal of U.S.-led forces. Taliban interlocutors have called for a pullback of foreign forces to their bases, followed by a cease-fire and a timetable for phased military withdrawal. They have offered to halt attacks against foreign and government troops as they leave.[5] In these and other ways Taliban representatives have shown a readiness to engage in a political bargaining process to achieve their primary purpose of removing foreign troops. U.S. military commanders have expressed support for negotiated solutions and have aided the passage of senior Taliban leaders to attend initial peace talks in Kabul.[6]

Former Taliban officials have said that they would be willing to cooperate in preventing the use of Afghan territory for planning and launching global terrorist attacks. Former Taliban ambassador to Pakistan Mullah Abdul Salam Zaeef told an interviewer in 2009 that "the United States has a right to guarantee its own security." Former Taliban foreign minister Mullah Wakil Ahmad Mutawakil acknowledged in the same interview that Americans have the right to "ensure there is no danger to them from Afghanistan."[7] Some Taliban leaders consider the movement's pre-2001 cozy relationship with al Qaeda a strategic blunder that led to their fall from power.[8] They are determined not to repeat that mistake in the future. If jettisoning links to al Qaeda and cooperating in suppressing terror strikes is necessary to secure the removal of foreign troops, many Taliban leaders would be willing to accept such a deal.

These are positive indications of a readiness by at least some Taliban notables to negotiate an agreement that addresses U.S. strategic interests as well as their own. Local cooperation in preventing global terrorist strikes would address the primary purpose of U.S. intervention in the region. Such an agreement would "constitute a strategic defeat for al Qaeda," according to Rubin and Rashid.[9] It would meet the priority U.S. and international security objective of countering global terrorist threats.

Reconciliation

Security cooperation in Afghanistan will be impossible without a political solution and reconciliation process within the country that leads to more inclusive and less corrupt national and local governance. The Afghanistan Study Group argues that a solution to the conflict depends on resolving the distribution of power among contending ethnic and political factions and between the central government and the provinces. A political solution is needed that balances the competing interests of the Tajik, Uzbek, and other Northern Alliance groups that dominate the Kabul government and the Pashtun groups that support the Taliban-led insurgency.

The need for some degree of reconciliation and power sharing between the Kabul regime and the Taliban has been acknowledged since the beginning of the conflict and is now official Afghan government policy. Much attention has been devoted to reconciliation efforts over the years, but little has been accomplished. The efforts to date have been half-hearted, under-resourced, and misdirected. The problems result from a flawed reconciliation strategy, a misguided belief in the efficacy of military coercion, and a lack of commitment from key officials in Washington and Kabul.

The logic of reconciliation is compelling. Armed conflicts end through either military victory or negotiated solutions that usually include some form of power sharing among former belligerents. Since the prospects of military victory for either side in Afghanistan are nil, a negotiated settlement is the only rational option. Afghan and foreign officials recognize this, but they have focused their reconciliation efforts on lower-level Taliban officials rather than the senior leaders who are directing the insurgency. U.S./NATO officials continue to insist that further military pressure is needed to bring the Taliban to the bargaining table, a belief that is naïve and counterproductive in the current setting. Certainly the balance of power in an armed conflict influences the outcome of negotiations, but the kind of military stalemate that prevails in Afghanistan does not confer political advantages for the United States. On the contrary, the continuation of war benefits the Taliban's strategy of protracted struggle. The result of foreign military action to date has been to strengthen the Taliban, not weaken it. The longer negotiations are delayed in favor of military action, the more difficult the bargaining will be, and the less incentive the Taliban will have to compromise.

Proposals for reconciliation began soon after the new Afghan government was installed. In 2002 the Karzai government offered amnesty to all members of the former regime, except for the 142 Taliban supporters named on the UN terrorism blacklist. The first talks between the Karzai government and Taliban representatives began as early as 2003, through contacts developed by UNAMA. These initial efforts produced meager results, however, because of a lack of sustained commitment from Afghan leaders and their Western backers. In 2005, the Kabul regime created the Peace Strengthening Commission as a vehicle for recruiting rank-and-file Taliban to the government side. By October 2006, 2,400 individuals signed letters foreswearing insurgency and agreeing to support the government. Of these, about 1,000 were former fighters, although very few were active commanders. The process was plagued by a lack of trust among the Taliban in the genuineness of the government's commitment to reconciliation.[10]

A blueprint for how to pursue dialogue with the Taliban has been developed by Michael Semple, former deputy for reconciliation to the European Union special representative in Afghanistan. In his book *Reconciliation in Afghanistan,* Semple draws from his years of experience in the reconciliation process to examine the history of failed attempts to date and the options for reaching a political settlement in the future. Semple notes that Taliban groups previously attempting to reintegrate with the new government were subjected to arbitrary arrest, seizure of assets, and general harassment. The chronology of nearly every regrouped Taliban network, writes Semple, includes the tale of how "their commanders were driven out of southern Afghanistan." These acts of repression occurred before the insurgency, not after. It was such mistreatment that drove many to armed revolt. From his direct experience in reconciliation efforts and interviews with two hundred Afghans who took part in the process, Semple concludes that U.S., Afghan, and international officials have been "singularly ill-equipped and often disinclined to take the needed steps to enable Afghans to reconcile and reintegrate peacefully back into society."[11]

Semple argues for direct talks with the Taliban leadership council in Quetta, Pakistan. The goal should be to negotiate a strategic agreement on renouncing international terrorism and integrating reconciled insurgents into the Afghan political system. The talks should seek commitments from militia leaders and tribal chiefs to cooperate in isolating al Qaeda and prevent their territory from being used for global terrorist strikes. Such a plan, if linked to the withdrawal of foreign forces, would have the support of many rank-and-file Taliban fighters. Leading military experts estimate that as many as 90 percent of Taliban fighters are reconcilable and could be co-opted politically with the right bargain.[12]

The Afghan government adopted a reconciliation strategy at the June 2010 peace jirga, but the plan lacks specifics and has serious shortcomings. Contradictions exist between the U.S. strategy, which demands preconditions and seeks to weaken the Taliban militarily before talks can begin, and the Karzai approach, which favors immediate direct negotiation. The Afghanistan Study Group argues that preconditions should not be imposed as a requirement for negotiation. Many Afghan and U.S. officials tend to view the challenge of reconciliation as a technical problem and have underestimated the powerful political and ideological motives that drive the insurgency. Thomas Ruttig and other analysts argue that economic and social incentives alone will not be sufficient. Inducing Taliban cooperation will require strategic concessions, including political power sharing and the disengagement of foreign troops. The peace jirga did not clarify these issues, in part because it lacked legitimacy and representativeness and was not preceded by sufficiently broad public consultation.[13]

The proposed reconciliation and negotiation process will not be successful without the participation of representatives from Afghanistan's broad and diverse array of civil society organizations and networks. The process must be based on genuine participation and buy-in from the Afghan people. Local and provincial as well as national leaders, both rural and urban, women and men, religious and secular, need places at the table. The participation of women is especially important in helping to ensure that the reconciliation process addresses the needs of Afghan families and communities, not just the interests of political leaders and militia commanders, and that the human rights advances of recent years are not abandoned in the interest of political compromise. Female participation should include not only government officials and members of parliament but also leaders and activists of community groups. Broadening participation in the national reconciliation process will help to produce a more widely supported and representative political settlement.

Demilitarization Strategy—Mutual Reinforcing Commitments

United States and Allies
- Begin military withdrawal
- Cease offensive operations and shift to civilian protection
- Support UN-brokered group of neighboring states
- Assemble and support temporary protection force
- Provide sustained support for development and human rights

Kabul Government
- Negotiate power sharing and political reconciliation with the Taliban
- Assure full participation of women and civil society in the reconciliation process
- Enforce constitutionally guaranteed rights
- Cooperate with temporary protection force
- Cooperate with UN-brokered group of neighboring states

Taliban
- Cease attacks
- Cooperate in suppressing al Qaeda
- Negotiate power sharing and political reconciliation with the Kabul government
- Integrate fighters into Afghan security forces
- Cooperate with temporary protection force

Decentralization

Selig Harrison argues that peace negotiations with the Taliban should focus less on Kabul and more on the provinces in the south and east that have been the traditional Taliban power base and are now largely under its control. The emphasis should shift from the terms of power sharing in Kabul to "the nature and degree of power to be ceded to the Taliban in its Pashtun strongholds."[14] In a recent article in *Foreign Affairs*, Stephen Biddle and other prominent Afghan experts argue for a related process of decentralizing political power in Afghanistan. The U.S. nation-building project in Afghanistan "no longer appears feasible, if it ever was," according to Biddle and his colleagues. The attempt to create a centralized state structure is "too radical a departure" in a country where localism and decentralization have been the traditional way of organizing political power. Shifting to a looser federated structure of power would return to the model that existed prior to the 1970s.

Throughout much of Afghan history, centralized governments have had "limited legitimacy and capacity."[15] They have lacked the ability to exert political control or deliver goods and services in many parts of the country. Kabul has ruled instead through bargains and power-sharing arrangements with local and regional leaders. Many communities in Afghanistan and the frontier regions of Pakistan have been self-governed for centuries by informal but robust tribal institutions. The idea of replacing these local governance systems with centralized rule from a Kabul government is alien and abhorrent to many rural Pashtuns. Attempted encroachments into the tribal regions in the past have often been a trigger for insurgency and violence. Over time the authority of Kabul has increased, but attempts to accelerate this trend have led to resistance. Many tribal communities are not willing to submit to externally driven attempts to create new forms of centralized government. Current efforts to establish such a system have not been successful and have contributed to the factors driving renewed insurgency.

Hamid Karzai is sometimes called "the mayor of Kabul." This is less an insult than an acknowledgment that the Afghan state over which he presides has little authority in most of the country. Kabul rules not through its own administration but through the power systems of appointed governors and local officials. Provincial leaders exercise authority not by virtue of the mandate from Kabul but on the basis of their own local militia forces and economic power bases.

Biddle and his colleagues argue that the United States should "step back from its ambitious, too unrealistic project" of creating a centralized state.[16] They recommend devolving most functions of government to local authorities, while preserving federal predominance in matters of security and foreign policy. This would open up a range of options for power sharing and decentralized governance and would make it easier to negotiate political arrangements with the Taliban and other insurgent groups. Harrison believes that Karzai might be willing to cede authority to the Taliban in Helmand, Khost, and other provinces where they are now dominant in return for holding on to power in Kabul. Such an approach would establish a political balance internally, while preserving Kabul's authority to cooperate in suppressing global terrorist threats.

Decentralization has its risks. Local governors would be free, as indeed they are now, to adopt regressive social policies that restrict women's rights and violate international human rights standards. In many local communities conservative elders and religious leaders already enforce rigid traditions and social practices that restrict options and opportunities for women. This was the case before the U.S.-led intervention and it remains the case today, especially in rural areas, despite the presence of 150,000 foreign troops. The ability of the United States and outside powers to influence political life and social practices in Afghanistan's thousands of local villages is extremely limited.

A devolution strategy does not mean abandoning human rights commitments, although it does acknowledge the limits of external influence. As noted, the United States and its partners will retain leverage by controlling the pace and scale of military withdrawals, and the level of financial assistance for the Kabul government. These forms of leverage can be used to encourage continued adherence to constitutionally guaranteed rights and progressive legislation such as the EVAW law. This will provide some protections for educated women in Kabul and other cities, but it will not affect life in remote villages that have never been nor likely ever will be subservient to the rule of Kabul or the preferences of foreign governments.

Peacemaking Diplomacy

The strategy of military disengagement for enhanced security must include a regional diplomatic initiative to constrain violent extremism and protect Afghanistan from foreign interference. Harrison argues that diplomatic cooperation among neighboring states is crucial to securing Afghanistan as foreign forces leave:

> Geopolitical arithmetic suggests an exit strategy that would contain Taliban influence after U.S. combat troops depart. Six of the seven neighboring regional powers with a stake in Afghanistan's future—Russia, Iran, India, China, Uzbekistan, and Tajikistan—share the U.S. goal of preventing the return of a Taliban dictatorship in Kabul.[17]

Four of these countries—Russia, Iran, India, and Tajikistan—cooperated with the United States in removing the Taliban regime in 2001. All are threatened by Muslim extremist movements that could be energized by the return of Taliban power in Kabul. It is precisely to avoid this eventuality that India and other neighboring countries are already heavily engaged in Afghanistan. This common regional interest needs to be harnessed and structured within a UN-managed diplomatic framework that prioritizes the security of Afghanistan and the stability of the region.

The Afghanistan Study Group recommends "an energetic diplomatic effort, spearheaded by the United Nations and strongly backed by the United States and its allies," to forge an agreement among regional powers for military neutralization and stabilization.[18] This will not be possible without a U.S. commitment to disengage militarily. The regional powers do not wish to legitimate an enduring U.S. military presence and will not cooperate in an arrangement in which Washington continues to dictate policy through military means. Proceeding with U.S. troop withdrawals will be necessary to gain the cooperation of neighboring states and to spark UN leadership into creating the needed regional compact. As Harrison notes, "Afghanistan's neighbors would be more likely to help contain the Taliban under a UN-brokered agreement than under wartime conditions in which they want to avoid identification with an unpopular U.S. military presence."[19]

The proposed diplomatic process for military neutralization would correspond to the recommended security agreement between Afghanistan and the United States. It would bar the use of Afghan territory, including Taliban-controlled areas, for transnational terrorist activities. It would establish limits on the size of Afghan security forces and prohibit all forms of foreign military involvement that are not approved by the Afghan government and the United Nations.

India and Pakistan

The key to neutralizing Afghanistan will be balancing the competing interests of India and Pakistan. India has attempted to exert major influence in Afghanistan since the fall of the Taliban.[20] Karzai and other senior Afghan officials have strong connections with India. New Delhi has invested hundreds of millions of dollars in humanitarian relief and infrastructure development projects.[21] India recently opened its first airbase on foreign soil in Tajikistan, partially to facilitate its involvement in Afghanistan. More than 4,000 Indians are now working in Afghanistan to complete infrastructure development projects and provide security assistance. India's major strategic objectives in Afghanistan include preventing the Taliban from regaining power, limiting Pakistan's influence in the region, and preventing the rise of Islamist extremist groups such as the Pakistan-based group Lashkar-e-Taiba, which perpetrated the bloody

November 2008 Mumbai attacks.[22] In support of these goals India will remain heavily engaged in Afghanistan as it seeks to suppress terrorist networks and constrain Pakistan's influence in the region.

Pakistan's interests are the opposite of India's. The two rivals have used Afghanistan, as they have Kashmir, as a proxy arena in which to assert their competing interests and struggle for advantage. The Pakistani government has long supported elements of the Taliban and various insurgent terrorist groups as a bulwark against Indian influence in Afghanistan and as a strategic wedge for influencing affairs in Kashmir. Pakistan's policy of supporting elements of the Taliban undermines security in Afghanistan and has backfired within Pakistan itself, where the Taliban has steadily gained influence. In 2009 the International Crisis Group reported an upsurge of jihadi violence not only in the Northwest Frontier Province (NWFP) and FATA region but also in Punjab and Baluchistan.[23] In response to this growing threat and the rising tide of terrorist attacks, the Pakistani army has responded with large-scale military operations in the NWFP and FATA territories, in a few cases leveling whole villages and generating large numbers of casualties and refugees. The army's heavy-handed methods have backfired and created resentments among local populations. Pakistani troops are mainly lowland Punjabis, culturally foreign to the northwest areas where they are operating and untrained in counterinsurgency. Army operations have angered many local Pashtun residents and contributed to a rejection response. U.S. drone attacks in the region have further enflamed militancy and generated additional support for anti-American insurgency.

Gaining Pakistani cooperation in preventing a Taliban takeover in Afghanistan will be difficult. Washington has designated Islamabad a strategic ally and over the past decade has pumped in some $20 billion in aid, much of it for the Pakistani military.[24] U.S. spending on Pakistani security forces is about $2 billion per year.[25] Yet the Pakistan government and armed forces continue to provide support for Taliban forces fighting U.S. troops in Afghanistan.

The proposed diplomatic compact may be the best option for gaining Pakistani cooperation. Islamabad might be willing to participate in a military neutralization agreement if it helps to bar India from direct military involvement in Afghanistan and limits its future influence. This would also be an incentive for the participation of China, which would provide some reassurance for Pakistan. Islamabad's participation also would be more likely if a political settlement within Afghanistan preserved influence for the Taliban in its Pashtun heartland adjacent to Pakistan. All of this would involve a delicate and uncertain balancing act, but a diplomatic initiative along these lines is essential for achieving security and stability in Afghanistan and the region.

Iran

The government of Iran has a long-standing policy of opposition to the Taliban. In the months after 9/11 Iran provided extensive assistance to the United States in overthrowing the Taliban regime in Afghanistan. Former ambassador James Dobbins, Washington's first envoy to the Karzai regime, has characterized this as "perhaps the most constructive period of U.S.-Iranian diplomacy since the fall of the Shah." During the Bonn conference, the United States worked closely with the Iranian delegation. "Iranian representatives were particularly helpful," wrote Dobbins. It was the Iranian delegate who first insisted that the Bonn agreement include a commitment to hold democratic elections in Afghanistan.[26]

This extensive Iranian cooperation in removing the Taliban regime was confirmed in 2005 by Mohsen Rezaie, then head of the Revolutionary Guards, who complained that the United States had not given Iran enough credit for its "important role in the overthrow of the Taliban" in 2001. Rezaie said that Revolutionary Guard troops advised and fought alongside Northern Alliance forces, playing a key role in the capture of Kabul.[27]

Iran does not want a return of Taliban rule, but it also opposes the presence of U.S. military forces on its borders. WikiLeaks documents depict Iranian intelligence agents providing cash and equipment to

Taliban fighters attacking U.S. troops. The documents confirm long-standing links between Iranian agents and Gulbuddin Hekmatyar, the former Afghan prime minister and notorious insurgent leader. Commanding General Stanley McChrystal asserted in May 2010 that Iran is providing training and weapons to Afghan insurgents but gave no concrete evidence. Earlier sources show no proof of shipments of arms from Iranian state agencies to insurgent groups in Afghanistan.[28]

The Tehran government has denied supporting the Taliban but may be playing a double game, supporting those who fight against U.S. forces while officially supporting the Kabul government. Preventing Taliban rule nonetheless remains an Iranian priority. Long-standing economic and political relations continue between Tehran and Kabul.

The United States and Iran share a common interest in opposing the Taliban and supporting a more stable and secure Afghanistan. By returning to the pattern of cooperation that existed in 2001 the two countries could help to achieve these goals and secure Afghanistan's future. Such cooperation could pay dividends in other diplomatic arenas, perhaps creating a basis for interaction and mutual understanding that might help to resolve the standoff over Tehran's nuclear program.

Responsibility and Risk

The United States owes a huge debt to the people of Afghanistan. This is not an excuse for maintaining an unwinnable war, but for ensuring that the United States makes an enduring commitment to development and democracy in Afghanistan, sustained well beyond the period of military disengagement. As Wildman and Bennis write, "Far from 'abandoning' the people of that war-torn country, a military withdrawal is the necessary first step toward a serious campaign of financial, development, humanitarian, environmental, and other kinds of reparations and reconstruction."[29] The United States and other donor states should empower the UN and other international development organizations to serve as the lead agencies in sustained programs of capacity building and improved democratic governance. The goal should be to channel as much funding as possible directly into Afghan hands, rather than through U.S. or other international contractors. This is especially true for programs to protect the rights of women. Support should be provided directly to Afghan women rather than through male-dominated military or government agencies.

Part of the U.S. responsibility in Afghanistan is to protect those who have collaborated with the U.S.-led intervention, and to provide sanctuary and support if this becomes necessary and is requested. This responsibility extends especially to the many aspiring women, particularly in Kabul, who have served in government or worked for international agencies and who are increasingly threatened because of their opposition to the Taliban and involvement with the international intervention. After 2001 many women cast their lot with the U.S.-led coalition and the Kabul regime, believing that they would end the Taliban nightmare and open new vistas of self-fulfillment and opportunity. Some of those hopes have been fulfilled, but many have been dashed as violence has increased and reactionary tendencies have strengthened. Western-oriented women are increasingly vulnerable to attack, and they could be further threatened and silenced as the Taliban gain greater influence in government. These women and the many thousands of people who have supported Western-backed reform in Afghanistan should not be abandoned as the United States and its allies begin to disengage militarily.

Providing sanctuary and relocation for exiles from Afghanistan poses enormous challenges. Attempting to ameliorate the consequences of past strategic mistakes is never easy or attractive. Political leaders prefer to proclaim military victory rather than explain the consequences of ambiguous military outcomes. In an era of political backlash against immigrants and Muslims, few countries will be eager to offer asylum to Afghan refugees. The moral responsibility is inescapable, however. Having intervened in their country, sowing the seeds of war and instability, the United States and its allies owe the Afghan people nothing less.

The proposed security and political strategies outlined here pose many risks and challenges. The required changes within Afghanistan and among its neighbors are daunting and fraught with uncertainty. An armed conflict that has continued as long as this one has becomes self-perpetuating. The participants gain a stake in preserving the power and economic benefits that flow from war. Factions within Afghanistan and among neighboring states have sharply different goals and interests, and will find it hard to agree. Many spoilers can be counted on to undermine the necessary political and military adjustments. The prospects for success are uncertain at best.

Military withdrawals will reduce the number of casualties, but this will not eliminate power struggles and the possibility of continued armed violence. Fierce competition over political power in Kabul and in the provinces may continue and intensify. The prospect of renewed civil war cannot be discounted. The vicious internal fighting and wanton attacks against civilians that characterized the civil war of 1992–1996 are sobering reminders of the potential for intensified violence and civilian suffering. Because of this history and the potential danger of renewed internal strife military disengagement must be carefully calibrated and staged gradually. The United States and its allies have a responsibility to manage their withdrawal in a manner that seeks stability and steers power struggles toward nonviolent forms.

The gains that have been achieved in social development and political rights for women are precarious and could be reversed. A political backlash by conservative factions has already developed in the Kabul government and parliament—this despite the presence of 100,000 U.S. troops and vast amounts of financial assistance. If political power sharing brings Taliban representation into government, reactionary trends will deepen. Political struggles over these issues will continue in Afghanistan. The U.S. ability to shape these events is limited now, and will diminish over time. Humility does not come easily to political leaders, but it is necessary when surveying the meager choices available.

As foreign forces leave, insurgent groups will claim victory and may gain temporary reputational advantage, as the mujahideen did in the late 1980s. This would not alter underlying political power relations, however, nor lead to a Taliban takeover. Afghan security forces and

Northern Alliance factions would retain superior military and political power. Opinion polls show that the Afghan people oppose the policies and practices of the Taliban and do not want their return to power. The Taliban benefits now from the aura of leading a national resistance against foreign forces, but when the intervention and insurgency end this advantage will erode. Deeply rooted revulsion at Taliban policies and methods will reemerge. The Taliban would have to gain political support by providing services in the communities they control. Given their dismal record in the past, it seems unlikely they could hold public support for very long.

The uncertainties are many, but the proposed strategy of gradual demilitarization offers the best option among limited and unattractive choices. Military disengagement will enable the United States and its allies to exert leverage for tangible security and political benefits while preventing the Taliban from regaining power. The current strategy of large-scale counterinsurgency and targeted bombing is questionable morally, unwinnable militarily, and unsustainable politically. The alternative may be risky, but it is preferable to the known dangers of war.

Notes

Introduction

1. Bob Woodward, *Obama's Wars* (New York: Simon & Schuster, 2010), 253, 260, 301, 320–21.

2. Joshua Partlow, "Karzai wants U.S. to reduce military operations in Afghanistan," *Washington Post,* November 14, 2010.

Chapter 1

1. Peter Bergen, "Winning the good war: why Afghanistan is not Obama's Vietnam," *Washington Monthly,* July/August 2009.

2. Michael Walzer, *Arguing about War* (New Haven: Yale University Press, 2004), 137. See also "Michael Walzer on Just War in Iraq," videotaped interview, available on *Big Think,* http://bigthink.com/michaelwalzer/michael -walzer-on-just-war-911-and-afghanistan (accessed June 15, 2009).

3. All citations from United States Conference of Catholic Bishops, "A Pastoral Message: Living with Faith and Hope After September 11," Washington, DC, November 14, 2001, http://www.usccb.org/sdwp/sept11.shtml.

4. Scott Simon, "Even pacifists must support this war," *Wall Street Journal,* October 11, 2001.

5. "Deny them their victory: a religious response to terrorism," *Sojourners* 30, no. 6 (November–December 2001): 26, http://www.sojo.net/index .cfm?action=magazine.article&issue=soj0111&article=011110e (accessed June 11, 2009).

6. "War in Afghanistan," editorial, *America* 185, no. 13 (October 29, 2001): 3, http://www.americamagazine.org/content/article.cfm?article_ id=1174 (accessed June 11, 2009).

7. Barbara Crossette, "U.S. steps up pressure on Taliban to deliver Osama bin Laden," *New York Times,* October 19, 1999.

8. Thomas Ruttig, *How Tribal Are the Taleban?: Afghanistan's Largest Insurgent Movement Between Its Tribal Roots and Islamist Ideology* (Afghanistan Analysts Network), AAN Thematic Report 04/2010, 17 (accessed May 12, 2009).

9. Barnett R. Rubin, interview by David Cortright and Linda Gerber, June 14, 2001, New York.

10. Doyle McManus, "From the start, Bush plan was to use the big stick," *Los Angeles Times,* October 9, 2001.

11. Duane Shank, "War in Afghanistan: was it just?" *Mennonite Life* 57, no. 1 (March 2002), available at Bethel College, http://www.bethelks.edu/mennonitelife/2002mar/shank_pf.php (accessed June 11, 2009).

12. Walzer, *Arguing about War,* ix.

13. National Conference of Catholic Bishops, *The Challenge of Peace: God's Promise and Our Response* (Washington, DC: United States Catholic Conference, 1983), par. 83.

14. Reinhold Niebuhr, "Why the Christian Church is not Pacifist," in *Christianity and Power Politics* (New York: Charles Scribner's Sons, 1940), 24.

15. On the question of militarization, see Admiral Mike Mullen, chairman of the Joint Chiefs of Staff, "Global Trends and National Security" (policy address, Woodrow Wilson School of Public and International Affairs, Princeton University, February 5, 2009), available at *Joint Chiefs of Staff,* http://www.jcs.mil/speech.aspx?ID=1128 (accessed June 8, 2009): "You've heard us, some of us and certainly me, talk about our foreign policy being too militarized. I believe that. And it's got to change." U.S. defense secretary Robert Gates recently referred to the "creeping militarization" of U.S. foreign policy. He described concerns about this trend as "not an entirely unreasonable sentiment." Robert M. Gates, "U.S. Global Leadership Campaign" (speech, Washington, DC, July 15, 2008), available at the *U.S. Department of Defense,* http://www.defenselink.mil/speeches/speech.aspx?speechid=1262 (accessed August 15, 2008).

16. John Rawls, *A Theory of Justice,* rev. ed. (Cambridge, MA: The Belknap Press of Harvard University Press, 1999), 335.

17. David Wildman and Phyllis Bennis, *Ending the US War in Afghanistan: A Primer* (Northampton, MA: Olive Branch Press, 2010), 17.

18. The White House, "U.S. National Security Strategy 2010" (Washington, DC, May 2010), 19–20, http://www.whitehouse.gov/sites/default/files/rss_viewer/national_security_strategy.pdf (accessed August 24, 2010).

19. The White House Interagency Policy Group, "White Paper of the

Interagency Policy Group's Report on U.S. Policy toward Afghanistan and Pakistan" (white paper, Washington, DC, March 2009), available at *The White House,* http://www.whitehouse.gov/assets/documents/Afghanistan -Pakistan_White_Paper.pdf (accessed June 11, 2009).

20. Ibid.

21. Lawrence Wright, "The rebellion within: An al Qaeda mastermind questions terrorism," *The New Yorker,* June 2, 2008, http://www.newyorker .com/reporting/2008/06/02/080602fa_fact_wright?currentPage=all (accessed June 15, 2009).

22. *A New Way Forward: Rethinking U.S. Strategy in Afghanistan,* Report of the Afghanistan Study Group, August 16, 2010, http://www .afghanistanstudygroup.com/.

23. Transcript of interview with CIA director Leon Panetta: Jake Tapper, "This Week," ABC News, June 27, 2010, http://abcnews.go.com/ThisWeek/ week-transcriptpanetta/story?id=11025299; see also "Leon Panetta: There may be less than 50 al Qaeda fighters in Afghanistan," *Huffington Post,* June 27, 2010, http://www.huffingtonpost.com/2010/06/27/leon-panetta-there -may-be_n_627012.html (accessed December 29, 2010).

24. George W. Bush, "Remarks by the President to the Warsaw Conference on Combatting Terrorism," The White House Press Office, November 6, 2001, http://georgewbush-whitehouse.archives.gov/news/ releases/2001/11/20011106-2.html (accessed June 3, 2010).

25. "CIA report into shoring up Afghan war support in Western Europe," WikiLeaks release, March 26, 2010, CIA Red Cell Special Memorandum; Afghanistan: Sustaining West European Support for the NATO-led Mission— Why Counting on Apathy Might Not Be Enough, http://mirror .wikileaks. info/leak/cia-afghanistan.pdf (accessed November 22, 2010).

26. Nicholas D. Kristof, "What about Afghan women?" *New York Times,* October 23, 2010.

27. International Commission on Intervention and State Sovereignty, *The Responsibility to Protect* (Ottawa: International Development Research Centre, December 2001), xii.

28. United Nations General Assembly, A More Secure World: Our Shared Responsibility, Report of the High-level Panel on Threats, Challenges and Change, A/59/565, New York, November 29, 2004, pars. 201 and 203.

29. United Nations Assistance Mission in Afghanistan, *Afghanistan Mid Year Report 2010, Protection of Civilians in Armed Conflict,* http://info .publicintelligence.net/UN-Afghan-Civilians-2010.pdf (accessed August 24, 2010).

30. United Nations Assistance Mission in Afghanistan, *Annual Report on Protection of Civilians in Armed Conflict, 2009* (Kabul: UNAMA, January 2010): 1, http://unama.unmissions.org/Portals/UNAMA/human%20rights/ Protection%20of%20Civilian%202009%20report%20English.pdf (accessed July 16, 2010).

31. This data is derived from the following sources: United Nations General Assembly and Security Council report of the Secretary-General, *The Situation in Afghanistan and Its Implications for International Peace and Security,* December 10, 2010, A/65/612-S/2010/630 (2010), par. 55; Kenneth Katzman, *Afghanistan: Post-Taliban Governance, Security, and U.S. Policy* (Washington, DC: Congressional Research Service, 2009), 50; United Nations Assistance Mission in Afghanistan, *Annual Report on Protection of Civilians in Armed Conflict, 2009,* executive summary; United Nations General Assembly and Security Council report of the Secretary-General, *The Situation in Afghanistan and Its Implications for International Peace and Security,* March 10, 2009, A/63/751-S/2009/135 (2009), 12–13, par. 66; United Nations General Assembly and Security Council report of the Secretary-General, *The Situation in Afghanistan and Its Implications for International Peace and Security,* March 6, 2008, A/62/722-S/2008/159 (2008), p. 4, par. 17; Human Rights Watch, "Troops in Contact: Airstrikes and Civilian Deaths in Afghanistan" (New York: Human Rights Watch, 2008): 13–14.

32. David Kilcullen, *The Accidental Guerrilla: Fighting Small Wars in the Midst of a Big One* (Oxford: Oxford University Press, 2009), xv, 259.

33. Michael Walzer, *Just and Unjust Wars: A Moral Argument with Historical Illustrations* (New York: Basic Books, 1977), 153–56.

34. Eric Schmitt, "Mindful of civilians, pilots in Afghanistan alter tactics," *New York Times,* July 14, 2009.

35. United Nations General Assembly and Security Council report of the Secretary-General, *The Situation in Afghanistan and Its Implications for International Peace and Security,* March 10, 2010, A/64/705-S/2010/127 (2010), 7, par. 24.

36. Ruttig, *How Tribal Are the Taleban?,* 17.

37. Afghanistan Rights Monitor, "The crisis of Afghan civilians in 2008," *Afghanistan Rights Monitor,* http://arm.org.af/index.php?page=en_ Latest+News+06 (accessed July 16, 2010).

38. Antonio Giustozzi, *Koran, Kalashnikov, and Laptop: The Neo-Taliban Insurgency in Afghanistan* (New York: Columbia University Press, 2008), 202.

39. The Rev. J. Bryan Hehir, "What can be done? What should be done?"

America 185, no. 10 (October 8, 2001): 9–12, http://www.americamagazine .org/content/article.cfm?article_id=1066 (accessed June 11, 2009).

40. Sir Ken Macdonald, director of public prosecutions, quoted in Clare Dyer, "There is no war on terror: outspoken DPP takes on Blair and Reid over fear-driven legal response to threat," *The Guardian,* January 24, 2007, 1, http:// www.guardian.co.uk/politics/2007/jan/24/uk.terrorism (accessed September 5, 2008).

41. Glenn L. Carle, "Overstating our fears," *Washington Post,* July 13, 2008.

42. Giustozzi, *Koran, Kalashnikov, and Laptop,* 216.

43. Seth G. Jones and Martin C. Libicki, *How Terrorist Groups End: Lessons for Countering al Qa'ida* (Santa Monica, CA: RAND Corporation, 2008), xiii–xiv, 42–43.

44. Francis Fukuyama, "After Neo-Conservatism," *New York Times Magazine,* February 19, 2006, 62.

45. Michael Scheuer, *Marching Toward Hell: America and Islam After Iraq* (New York: Free Press, 2008), 155. See also, for example, Dr. Steven Kull, director, Program on International Policy Attitudes (PIPA), "Negative Attitudes Toward the United States in the Muslim World: Do They Matter?" (testimony before House Committee on Foreign Affairs, Subcommittee on International Organizations, Human Rights, and Oversight, 110th Cong., 1st sess., Washington, DC, May 17, 2007), available at *World Public Opinion.org ,* http://www.worldpublicopinion.org/pipa/articles/brmiddleeastnafricara/361 .php?lb=btvoc&pnt=361&nid=&id= (accessed June 11, 2009). Dr. Kull referenced a recent poll conducted by PIPA that indicated that, among those polled in four Muslim countries, "8 in 10 believe that the U.S. seeks to 'weaken and divide the Islamic world.'"

46. Kilcullen, *Accidental Guerrilla,* 37.

47. Wildman and Bennis, *Ending the US War in Afghanistan,* 2.

48. Kilcullen, *Accidental Guerrilla,* 29, 264.

49. Gilles Dorronsoro, "Focus and Exit: An Alternative Strategy for the Afghan War" (position paper, Carnegie Endowment for International Peace, January 2009, Washington, DC), 9, 13.

50. Graham E. Fuller, "Obama worsening Afghan-Pak state," *Saudi Gazette,* May 11, 2009.

51. Giustozzi, *Koran, Kalashnikov, and Laptop,* 190.

52. Kilcullen, *Accidental Guerrilla,* 263, xiv, 85.

53. Steven Simon, "Can the right war be won? Defining American interests in Afghanistan," *Foreign Affairs* 88, no. 4 (July/August 2009): 136–37.

54. Selig S. Harrison, "Pakistan: The State of the Union" (special report, Center for International Policy, Washington, DC, April 2009), 32.

55. Christian Caryl, "Why they do it," *The New York Review of Books* 52, no. 14 (September 22, 2005).

56. Robert A. Pape and James K. Feldman, *Cutting the Fuse: The Explosion of Global Suicide Terrorism and How to Stop It* (Chicago: University of Chicago Press, 2010).

57. United Nations General Assembly, *Uniting Against Terrorism*, A/60/825, 27 April 2006, par. 28.

58. Dorronsoro, "Focus and Exit: An Alternative Strategy for the Afghan War," 2.

59. John Howard Yoder, *The Politics of Jesus*, 2d ed. (Grand Rapids, MI: Eerdmans, 1994), 204.

60. Robert C. Johansen, "Enforcement without Military Combat: Toward an International Civilian Police," in *Globalization and Global Governance*, ed. Raimo Väyrynen, 173–98 (Lanham, MD: Rowman and Littlefield, 1999).

61. For a critical analysis of the UN counterterrorism program, see Cortright et al., "Global cooperation against terrorism: Evaluating the United Nations Counter-Terrorism Committee," in *Uniting Against Terror: Cooperative Nonmilitary Responses to the Global Terrorist Threat,* David Cortright and George A. Lopez, eds., 23–50 (Cambridge, MA: MIT Press, 2007); see also Eric Rosand and Alistair Millar, "Strengthening International Law and Global Implementation," in *Uniting Against Terror,* Cortright and Lopez, eds., 51–82; and Cortright et al., "Strategies and Policy Challenges for Winning the Fight Against Terrorism," in *Uniting Against Terror,* Cortright and Lopez, eds., 237–74.

62. Robin Wright, "Invisible war on terror accelerates worldwide," *Los Angeles Times,* January 7, 2002.

Chapter 2

1. Sean Rayment, "General Sir David Richards: Why we cannot defeat al-Qaeda," *The Telegraph,* November 14, 2010, http://www.telegraph.co.uk/news/newstopics/politics/defence/8131217/General-Sir-David-Richards-Why-we-cannot-defeat-al-Qaeda.html (accessed November 15, 2010).

2. United Sates Interagency Counterinsurgency Initiative, *U.S. Government Counterinsurgency Guide* (Washington, DC: Bureau of Political-Military Affairs, January 2009), 3.

3. David Galula, *Counterinsurgency Warfare: Theory and Practice* (1964; repr., Westport, CT: Praeger Security International, 2006), 63.

4. Amy Belasco, "The Cost of Iraq, Afghanistan and Other Global War on Terror Operations," Congressional Research Service, May 15, 2009, 4, http://www.fas.org/sgp/crs/natsec/RL33110.pdf (accessed August 25, 2010); Cost of War Counter, National Priorities Project, August 12, 2009, http://www.costofwar.com/ (accessed August 25, 2010); Karen De Young and Greg Jaffe, "U.S. ambassador seeks more money for Afghanistan," *Washington Post,* August 12, 2009.

5. Tom Coghlan, "Afghan military strategy doomed without big changes, UN Chief warns," *The Times* (London), January 28, 2010, http://www.timesonline.co.uk/tol/news/world/afghanistan/article7005380.ece (accessed January 28, 2010).

6. Charles M. Sennott, "The Petraeus Doctrine," *The Boston Globe,* January 28, 2007.

7. Antonio Giustozzi, *Koran, Kalashnikov, and Laptop: The Neo-Taliban Insurgency in Afghanistan* (New York: Columbia University Press, 2008), 195, 214.

8. General Stanley McChrystal, "Commander's Initial Assessment," August 30, 2009. Commander, NATO International Security Assistance Force, Afghanistan, and US Forces, Afghanistan, http://media.washingtonpost.com/wpsrv/politics/documents/Assessment_Redacted_092109.pdf (accessed September 24, 2009).

9. Edward Epstein, "Success in Afghan war hard to gauge," March 23, 2002, *San Francisco Examiner,* http://www.globalsecurity.org/org/news/2002/020323-attack01.htm (accessed November 16, 2010).

10. Erica Gaston, Jonathan Horowitz, and Susanne Schmeidl, *Strangers at the Door: Night Raids by International Forces Lose Hearts and Minds of Afghans,* Open Society Institute and The Liaison Office Report, February 23, 2010.

11. Marika Theros and Mary Kaldor, "Building Afghan Peace from the Ground Up," unpublished draft paper, November 15, 2010.

12. David C. Gompert and John Gordon IV, with Adam Grissom et al., *War by Other Means: Building Complete and Balanced COIN Capabilities* (RAND Corporation, 2008), xxv, xlviii, http://www.rand.org/pubs/monographs/2008/RAND_MG595.2.pdf (accessed August 20, 2010).

13. Martin van Creveld, *The Changing Face of War: Combat from the Marne to Iraq* (New York: Ballantine, 2008), 268.

14. Giustozzi, *Koran, Kalashnikov, and Laptop,* 215–216.

15. Andrew J. Enterline and Joseph Magagnoli, "Reversal of Fortune? Strategy Change and Counterinsurgency Success by Foreign Powers in the Twentieth Century," http://www.psci.unt.edu/enterline/em-freshlook-v58 -identified.pdf (accessed June 22, 2010).

16. Colin H. Kahl, Brain Katulis, and Marc Lynch, "Thinking strategically about Iraq: report from a symposium," *Middle East Policy* 15, no. 1 (Spring 2008): 82–110.

17. Steve Simon, "The price of the surge: how U.S. strategy is hastening Iraq's demise," *Foreign Affairs* 87, no. 3 (May/June 2008): 57–67.

18. David Kilcullen, *The Accidental Guerrilla: Fighting Small Wars in the Midst of a Big One* (Oxford: Oxford University Press, 2009), 183.

19. See Leila Fadel, "Security in Iraq still elusive," *McClatchey Newspapers,* September 9, 2007, http://www.mcclatchydc.com/iraq/story/19566.html (accessed June 16, 2009).

20. Bernard Stancati, "Tribal dynamics and the Iraq surge," *Strategic Studies Quarterly* 4, no. 2 (Summer 2010), 95.

21. Seth G. Jones and Martin C. Libicki, *How Terrorist Groups End: Lessons for Countering al Qa'ida* (Santa Monica, CA: RAND Corporation, 2008), 89–90.

22. Jones and Libicki, *How Terrorist Groups End,* 97.

23. Kilcullen, *Accidental Guerrilla,* 179, 271.

24. Stancati, "Tribal Dynamics and the Iraq Surge," 95.

25. Gilles Dorronsoro, "Focus and Exit: An Alternative Strategy for the Afghan War" (position paper, Carnegie Endowment for International Peace, January 2009, Washington, DC), 6.

26. Kilcullen, *Accidental Guerrilla,* 111, 48.

27. Thomas Ruttig, *How Tribal Are the Taleban?: Afghanistan's Largest Insurgent Movement Between Its Tribal Roots and Islamist Ideology* (Afghanistan Analysts Network), AAN Thematic Report 04/2010, 1–3.

28. Selig S. Harrison, "Pakistan: The State of the Union" (special report, Center for International Policy, Washington, DC, April 2009), 33.

29. Ruttig, *How Tribal Are the Taleban?,* 1–3.

30. Jason Burke, "Misreading the Taliban," *Prospect Magazine* no. 152 (November 2008), quoted in Ruttig, *How Tribal Are the Taleban?,* 18.

31. Shibley Telhami, *The Stakes: America and the Middle East,* updated ed. (Boulder, CO: Westview Press, 2004), 28.

32. Ruttig, *How Tribal Are the Taleban?,* 2, 11.

33. Giustozzi, *Koran, Kalashnikov, and Laptop,* 39, 230.

34. Ibid., 40–41.

35. Kilcullen, *Accidental Guerrilla*, 58.

36. Giustozzi, *Koran, Kalashnikov, and Laptop*, 39, 111.

37. Washington Report on Middle East Affairs, "Human Rights: Perspectives of Afghan Women Leaders," *Washington Report on Middle East Affairs* (August 2010), http://www.washington-report.org/component/content/article/357/9705-human-rights-perspectives-of-afghan-women-leaders.html (accessed September 7, 2010).

38. Giustozzi, *Koran, Kalashnikov, and Laptop*, 42, 60, 69, 174-76.

39. Matt Waldman, "Dangerous Liaisons with the Afghan Taliban: The Feasibility and Risks of Negotiation," United States Institute of Peace, Special Report 256, October 2010.

40. Ambassador Karl W. Eikenberry, "COIN Strategy: Civilian Concerns," United States Department of State cable, Kabul 3572 (November 6, 2009), 2 (of 4), http://documents.nytimes.com/eikenberry-s-memos-on-the-strategy-in-afghanistan#document/p3 (accessed August 6, 2010).

41. Kilcullen, *Accidental Guerrilla*, 46, 105–110, 232.

42. Gompert and Gordon, with Grissom et al., *War by Other Means*, xxiv–v, http://www.rand.org/pubs/monographs/2008/RAND_MG595.2.pdf (accessed August 6, 2010).

43. Barbara Crossette, "Lakhdar Brahimi," *The Nation*, December 29, 2008, http://www.thenation.com/article/q-and-lakhdar-brahimi-what-next-gaza (accessed October 7, 2010).

44. Giustozzi, *Koran, Kalashnikov, and Laptop*, 16, 19.

45. Theros and Kaldor, "Building Afghan Peace from the Ground Up."

46. Ibid., 175–80.

47. Ibid., 215.

48. *A New Way Forward: Rethinking U.S. Strategy in Afghanistan*, Report of the Afghanistan Study Group, August 16, 2010, http://www.afghanistanstudygroup.com/.

49. David Wildman and Phyllis Bennis, *Ending the U.S. War in Afghanistan: A Primer* (Northampton, MA: Olive Branch Press, 2010), 156.

50. Kilcullen, *Accidental Guerrilla*, 48–49.

51. Giustozzi, *Koran, Kalashnikov, and Laptop*, 233.

52. Sean Rayment, "General Sir David Richards: Why we cannot defeat al-Qaeda."

53. Rory Stewart, "The irresistible illusion," *London Review of Books*, July 9, 2009, http://www.lrb.co.uk/v31/n13/stew01_.html (accessed September 22, 2009).

54. Kilcullen, *Accidental Guerrilla*, 52.

55. Bob Woodward, *Obama's Wars* (New York: Simon & Schuster, 2010), 302–3.

56. Giustozzi, *Koran, Kalashnikov, and Laptop,* 27, 35.

57. The White House, *Report on Afghanistan and Pakistan, September 2010,* 9–10, http://www.pbs.org/newshour/world/july-dec10/afghanpakistan0910 .pdf (accessed October 7, 2010).

58. United States Government Accountability Office, *Combating Terrorism: U.S. Efforts to Address the Terrorist Threat in Pakistan's Federally Administered Tribal Areas Require a Comprehensive Plan and Continued Oversight,* GAO-08-820T, May 20, 2008.

59. The White House, *Report on Afghanistan and Pakistan,* September 2010, 11.

60. Mark Mazzetti and Eric Schmidt, "C.I.A. steps up drone attacks on Taliban in Pakistan," *New York Times,* September 27, 2010, http://www .nytimes.com/2010/09/28/world/asia/28drones.html.

61. Helene Cooper and Eric Schmidt, "U.S. tries to calm Pakistan's anger over airstrike," *New York Times,* October 7, 2010, A11.

62. "Pakistan keeps border crossing shut," *Al Jazeera,* October 7, 2010, http://english.aljazeera.net/news/asia/2010/10/20101078849195792.html (accessed October 8, 2010).

Chapter 3

1. Deniz Kandiyoti, ed., *Women, Islam and the State* (Philadelphia: Temple University Press, 1991), 3–4.

2. Ahmed Rashid, *Taliban: Militant Islam, Oil, and Fundamentalism* (New Haven, CT: Yale University Press, 2000), 69. Rashid notes that during the 1990s, Hazara women were politically active, headed aid programs, and even fought the Taliban alongside their men.

3. Ibid., 23, 70, 108, 111–112.

4. Elaheh Rostami-Povey, *Afghan Women: Identity and Invasion* (London: Zed Books, Ltd, 2007), 28–38.

5. Peter S. Hill, Ghulam Farooq Mansoor, and Fernanda Claudio, "Conflict in least-developed countries: challenging the millennium development goals," *Bulletin of the World Health Organization* 88, no. 8 (August 2010): 562, http://www.who.int/bulletin/volumes/88/8/09-071365/en/index .html (accessed October 3, 2010).

6. Womankind Worldwide, "Taking stock update: Afghan women and

girls seven years on" (July 2008): 46, http://www.womankind.org.uk/upload/Taking%20Stock%20Report%2068p.pdf (accessed October 3, 2010).

7. Sheena Currie, Pashtoon Azfar, and Rebecca C. Flower, "A bold new beginning for midwifery in Afghanistan," *Midwifery* 23 (2007): 226, 229–230, http://www.amddprogram.org/conference/assets/Resources/Day%202/Global%20Exeperience/Currie%20et%20al_Midwives%20in%20Afghanistan_Midwifery_2007.pdf (accessed 3 October 2010).

8. Rosemarie Skaine, *Women in Afghanistan in the Post-Taliban Era: How Lives Have Changed and Where They Stand Today* (Jefferson, NC: McFarland and Company, 2008), 105.

9. Hill, Mansoor, and Claudio, "Conflict in least-developed countries," 562.

10. Ministry of Education, Islamic Republic of Afghanistan, Education Sector Strategy for the Afghanistan National Development Strategy (March 2007), http://planipolis.iiep.unesco.org/upload/Afghanistan/Afghanistan_MoE_strategy_English.pdf (accessed June 12, 2010).

11. United Nations Assistance Mission in Afghanistan, *Afghan Update, no. 23* (Summer 2010): Foreword, http://unama.unmissions.org/LinkClick.aspx?link=Afghan+Update/AU+Education+English+No.+23.pdf&tabid=1741&mid=3608 (accessed October 4, 2010).

12. National Democratic Institute for International Affairs, "The September 2005 Parliamentary and Provincial Council Elections in Afghanistan" (2005): 9, http://www.ndi.org/files/2004_af_report_041006.pdf (accessed July 1, 2010).

13. Jan Goodwin, *Price of Honor: Muslim Women Lift the Veil of Silence on the Islamic World* (New York: Plume, 2002), 87.

14. Elaheh Rostami Povery, "Women in Afghanistan, passive victims of the *borga* or active social participants?," *Farzaneh* 6, no. 11 (2003): 8, http://www.farzanehjournal.com/archive/Download/arti2n11.pdf (accessed October 4, 2010).

15. Amnesty International, "Women in Afghanistan: a Human Rights Catastrophe" (November 1995), http://www.amnesty.org/en/library/asset/ASA11/003/1995/en/942a70a6-eb60-11dd-b8d6-03683db9c805/asa110031995en.pdf (accessed June 10, 2010).

16. Radhika Coomaraswamy, "Integration of the Human Rights of Women and the Gender Perspective: Violence Against Women," *UN Economic and Social Council*, E/CN.4/2000/68/Add.4 13 (March 2000): 6–7.

17. Julie A. Mertus, *Wars Offensive on Women: The Humanitarian Challenges in Bosnia, Kosovo, and Afghanistan* (Bloomfield, CT: Kumarian Press, 2000), 58.

18. Coomaraswamy, "Integration of the Human Rights of Women and the Gender Perspective," 10.

19. Rosemarie Skaine, *The Women of Afghanistan Under the Taliban* (Jefferson, NC: McFarland, 2002), 69.

20. Human Rights Watch, "Afghanistan. Humanity Denied: Systematic Denial of Women's Rights in Afghanistan," Vol. 13, no. 5 (October 2001): 6–8.

21. Report of the Secretary General, "Discrimination against women and girls in Afghanistan," Commission on the Status of Women (March 2002): 6, http://www.angel-invest.us/events/women/2002/ecn620025eng.pdf (accessed June 10, 2010).

22. Human Rights Watch, "'Killing you is a very easy thing for us,' Human Rights Abuses in Southeast Afghanistan," Vol. 15, no. 5 (July 28, 2003): 27–29, http://www.hrw.org/en/reports/2003/07/28/killing-you-very-easy-thing-us-0 (accessed October 4, 2010).

23. International Organization for Migration, "Trafficking in human beings in Afghanistan: field survey report" (June 2008): 21–26, http://www.iom.int/jahia/webdav/shared/shared/mainsite/activities/countries/docs/afghanistan/iom_report_trafficking_afghanistan.pdf (accessed June 14, 2010).

24. Women for Women International, "2009 Afghanistan report: Amplifying the voices of women in Afghanistan," *Stronger Women, Stronger Nations Report Series* (2009): 26–27, http://www.womenforwomen.org/news-women-for-women/files/AfghanistanReport.FINAL.hi-res.pdf (accessed October 3, 2010).

25. UNICEF, "Early marriage: child spouses," *Innocenti Digest* #7 (March 2001): 4, http://www.unicef-irc.org/publications/pdf/digest7e.pdf (accessed June 10, 2010).

26. Skaine, *Women in Afghanistan in the Post-Taliban Era*, 68.

27. Takhmina Shokirova, Master Thesis, "Is Peace Achievable for Women: Comparative Study of Gender Relations in Private Sphere in Azerbaijan, Kyrgyzstan and Tajikistan," submitted to the University of Notre Dame in the fulfillment of Master Degree in Peace Studies (April 2010), 69.

28. UNICEF, "Early marriage: child spouses," *Innocenti Digest* #7 (March 2001): 6, http://www.unicef-irc.org/publications/pdf/digest7e.pdf (accessed June 10, 2010).

29. Rachel Reid, *We Have the Promises of the World: Women Rights in Afghanistan* (New York: Human Rights Watch, December 2009): 58, http://www.hrw.org/en/reports/2009/12/03/we-have-promises-world-0 (accessed May 28, 2010).

30. Max Planck Institute for Foreign Private Law and Private International

Law, "Family Structures and Family Law in Afghanistan, a Report of the Fact-Finding Mission to Afghanistan" (January–March 2005): 18, http://www.mpipriv.de/shared/data/pdf/mpi-report_on_family_structures_and_family_law_in_afghanistan.pdf (accessed June 10, 2010).

31. Hafizullah Emadi, *Repression, Resistance, and Women in Afghanistan* (Westport, CT: Praeger Security International, 2002), 30–31.

32. John R. Acerra, Kara Iskyan, Zubair A. Qureshi, and Rahul K. Sharma, "Rebuilding the health care system in Afghanistan: an overview of primary care and emergency services," *International Journal of Emergency Medicine* (2009): 77–82, http://www.springerlink.com/content/w6480w571654035x/fulltext.pdf (accessed September 2, 2010).

33. Currie, Azfar, and Flower, "A bold new beginning for midwifery in Afghanistan," 226–227.

34. United Nations Secretariat, Population Division of the Department of Economic and Social Affairs, "World population prospects: the 2008 revision" (2009): 41, http://www.un.org/esa/population/publications/wpp2008/wpp2008_text_tables.pdf (accessed October 4, 2010).

35. Linda A. Barlett, et al., "Maternal mortality in Afghanistan: magnitude, causes, risk factors and preventability" (Afghanistan Ministry of Public Health, CDC, UNICEF, 2002): 4.

36. United Nations Secretariat, Population Division of the Department of Economic and Social Affairs, "Total fertility rate (children per woman)," *UNdata,* http://data.un.org/Data.aspx?q=fertility+rate&d=PopDiv&f=variableID%3a54 (accessed August 2, 2010).

37. Womankind Worldwide, "Taking stock update," 45.

38. Hill, Mansoor, and Claudio, "Conflict in least-developed countries," 562.

39. Afghanistan Central Statistics Office, "Multiple indicator cluster survey findings," received from UNICEF office in Afghanistan, provided by Farid Dasgeer.

40. Skaine, *Women in Afghanistan in the Post-Taliban Era,* 105.

41. World Bank, "Afghanistan: national reconstruction and poverty reduction–the role of women in Afghanistan's future" (March 2005): 24, http://siteresources.worldbank.org/AFGHANISTANEXTN/Resources/AfghanistanGenderReport.pdf (accessed October 3, 2010).

42. Currie, Azfar, and Flower, "A bold new beginning for midwifery in Afghanistan," 229–230.

43. Womankind Worldwide, "Taking stock update: Afghan women and girls seven years on," 46.

44. National Action Plan for the Women of Afghanistan (NAPWA) for 2007–2017, 75–78.

45. Julius Cavendish, "Rough roads to better care," *Bulletin of the World Health Organization* 88, no. 8 (August 2010): 566–67, http://www.scielosp.org/pdf/bwho/v88n8/05.pdf (accessed October 3, 2010).

46. Skaine, *Women in Afghanistan in the Post-Taliban Era,* 68–69.

47. Stephen Biddle, Fotini Christia, and J. Alexander Thier, "Defining success in Afghanistan: what can the United States accept?" *Foreign Affairs* 89, no. 4 (July/August 2010): 54, http://www.foreignaffairs.com/articles/66450/stephen-biddle-fotini-christia-and-j-alexander-thier/defining-success-in-afghanistan (accessed October 3, 2010).

48. Reid, *We Have the Promises of the World,* 16.

49. World Bank, "Independent Impact Evaluation: National Solidarity Program Enhances Local Governance and Increases Involvement of Women" (May 2010), http://www.worldbank.org.af/WBSITE/EXTERNAL/COUNTRIES/SOUTHASIAEXT/AFGHANISTANEXTN/0,,contentMDK:22573708~menuPK:305990~pagePK:2865066~piPK:2865079~theSitePK:305985,00.html (accessed July 4, 2010).

50. Ibid.

51. Ximena Arteaga, "Assessing the demands for saving services among microfinance clients in Afghanistan," *Microfinance Investment Facility of Afghanistan—MISFA* (October 2009): iv, http://www.misfa.org.af/pdf/Savings%20Demand%20Study.pdf (accessed June 20, 2010).

52. Ibid., 22.

53. Antonio Donini, Norah Niland, and Karin Wermester, *Nation Building Unraveled?: Aid, Peace and Justice in Afghanistan* (Bloomfield, CT: Kumarin Press, 2004), 95.

54. Eric Lyby, "Microfinance and gender roles in Afghanistan", *World Bank Working Paper* (November 2006): 1, http://www.wds.worldbank.org/external/default/main?pagePK=64193027&piPK=64187937&theSitePK=523679&menuPK=64187510&searchMenuPK=64187283&theSitePK=523679&entityID=000310607_20061206142023&searchMenuPK=64187283&theSitePK=523679 (accessed July 4, 2010).

55. Microfinance Investment Facility for Afghanistan, "Gender mainstreaming in microfinance: making a positive impact on the lives of Afghan women" (June 2009), http://www.misfa.org.af/file.php?id=25 (accessed June 27, 2010).

56. Lyby, "Microfinance and gender roles in Afghanistan," 1–2.

57. Donini, Niland, and Wermester, *Nation Building Unraveled?,* 96.

58. United Nations Development Programme, "Human development index 2007 and its components: education index" (2009), http://hdrstats.undp.org/en/indicators/93.html (accessed June 8, 2010).

59. United Nations Development Fund for Women, "UNIFEM Afghanistan Fact Sheet 2008: The situation of women in Afghanistan," http://www.unifem.org/afghanistan/media/pubs/08/factsheet.html#education (accessed August 2, 2010).

60. World Bank, "Afghanistan: national reconstruction and poverty reduction—the role of women in Afghanistan's future" (March 2005): 31, http://siteresources.worldbank.org/AFGHANISTANEXTN/Resources/AfghanistanGenderReport.pdf (accessed October 3, 2010).

61. Skaine, *Women in Afghanistan in the Post-Taliban Era*, 68.

62. United Nations Assistance Mission in Afghanistan, *Afghan Update*, no. 23, Foreword.

63. USAID, "Afghanistan: education", Factsheet (June 2010), http://afghanistan.usaid.gov/en/Program.23a.aspx (accessed September 14, 2010).

64. World Bank, "World Bank indicators: ratio of female to male secondary enrollment," http://data.worldbank.org/indicator/SE.ENR.SECO.FM.ZS (accessed May 14, 2010).

65. Marit Glad, "Knowledge on fire: attacks on education in Afghanistan," CARE (November 2009): 25, 35–36, http://www.care.org/newsroom/articles/2009/11/Knowledge_on_Fire_Report.pdf (accessed March 31, 2010).

66. Reid, *We Have the Promises of the World*, 78.

67. Glad, "Knowledge on fire: attacks on education in Afghanistan," 25.

68. Human Rights Watch, "The 'ten-dollar Talib' and women's rights: Afghan women and the risk of reintegration and reconsiliation (July 13, 2010): 32, http://www.hrw.org/node/91466 (accessed September 25, 2010).

69. Antonio Giustozzi, *Koran, Kalashnikov, and Laptop: The Neo-Taliban Insurgency in Afghanistan* (New York: Columbia University Press, 2008), 104.

70. Glad, "Knowledge on fire: attacks on education in Afghanistan," 21.

71. Cited in Nicholas D. Kristof, "Dr. Greg and Afghanistan," *New York Times*, October 21, 2010, A31.

72. Giustozzi, *Koran, Kalashnikov, and Laptop*, 10.

73. Said Mahmoudi, "The *Shari'a* in the new Afghan constitution: contradiction or compliment?" *ZaöRV*, 64 (2004): 870–871, http://www.mpil.de/shared/data/pdf/mahmoudi,_the_shari%27a_in_the_new_afghan_constitution_contradiction_or_compliment.pdf (accessed October 3, 2010).

74. Masuda Sultan, "From rhetoric to reality: Afghan women on the agenda

for peace," Women Waging Peace, Policy Commission (February 2005): xi, http://www.huntalternatives.org/download/18_from_rhetoric_to_reality_ afghan_women_on_the_agenda_for_peace.pdf (accessed October 3, 2010).

75. Reid, *We Have the Promises of the World*, 5, 15–16.

76. International Crisis Group, "Afghanistan: women and reconstruction," *ICG Asia Report N 48* (March 14, 2003): i, http://www.crisisgroup.org/~/ media/Files/asia/south-asia/afghanistan/048%20-%20Afghanistan%20-% 20Women%20and%20Reconstruction.ashx (accessed October 3, 2010).

77. Human Rights Watch, "The 'ten-dollar Talib' and women's rights," 22.

78. Ministry of Women Affairs of Afghanistan, "National Action Plan for the Women of Afghanistan (NAPWA) for 2007–2017" (brochure).

79. The Asia Foundation, "Women participation in election," http:// asiafoundation.org/resources/pdfs/WEPelections.pdf (accessed July 1, 2010).

80. National Democratic Institute for International Affairs, "Afghanistan: the participation of women in 2009 elections," http://www.ndi.org/node/15752 (accessed July 1, 2010).

81. National Democratic Institute for International Affairs, "The September 2005 parliamentary and provincial council elections in Afghanistan" (2005): 9, http://www.ndi.org/files/2004_af_report_041006.pdf (accessed July 1, 2010).

82. UNIFEM, "Afghan women and the elections 1388" (2009), http:// www.unifem.org/afghanistan/media/events/2009/elections.html (accessed July 4, 2010).

83. Sarah Smiles Persinger, Interview with Sharif Nasry, Kabul, Afghanistan, May 2010.

84. Human Rights Watch, "Afghanistan: unchecked violence threatens election" (September 9, 2010), http://www.hrw.org/en/news/2010/09/09/ afghanistan-unchecked-violence-threatens-election (accessed September 25, 2010).

85. The Free and Fair Election Foundation of Afghanistan (FEFA), "First observation report of the 2010 Election Observation Mission: nomination of candidates" (June 16, 2010), http://fefa2010.wordpress.com/2010/06/16/ first-observation-report-of-the-2010-election-observation-missionnomination -of-candidates/ (accessed September 25, 2010).

86. Jon Boone, "Afghanistan election fraud fears force 900 polling stations to stay shut," *The Guardian* (August 17, 2010), http://www.guardian.co .uk/world/2010/aug/17/afghanistan-election-polling-stations-shut (accessed September 25, 2010).

87. National Democratic Institute for International Affairs, "The September 2005 parliamentary and provincial council elections in Afghanistan" (2005): 12, http://www.ndi.org/files/2004_af_report_041006.pdf (accessed October 4, 2010).

88. The Free and Fair Election Foundation of Afghanistan (FEFA), "First observation report of the 2010 Election Observation Mission: nomination of candidates."

89. Anna Wordsworth, "Moving to the mainstream: integrating gender in Afghanistan's national policy," Afghanistan Research and Evaluation Unit (February 2008): 26, 54. http://www.afghanconflictmonitor.org/2008/03/integrating-gen.html (accessed 3 October 2010).

90. Torunn Wimpelmann Chaudhary, Orzala Ashraf Nemat, and Astri Suhrke, "Afghanistan," in Ole Jacob Sending, ed. *Learning to Build Sustainable Peace: Ownership and Everyday Peacebuilding Legislation, Women's Rights and Obligations in Afghanistan*, Norwegian Institute of International Affairs (2010): 7, http://www.cmi.no/publications/file/3732-learning-to-build-a-sustainable-peace.pdf (accessed October 3, 2010).

91. "Power grab," *New York Times*, Editorial (February 23, 2010), http://www.nytimes.com/2010/02/24/opinion/24wed2.html (accessed July 6, 2010).

92. Joshua Partlow, "Afghanistan's government seeks more control over elections," *Washington Post* (February 15, 2010), http://www.washingtonpost.com/wp-dyn/content/article/2010/02/14/AR2010021401698.html (accessed July 6, 2010).

93. Alissa J. Rubin, "Karzai government re-writes key election law," *Boston Globe* (February 24, 2010), http://www.boston.com/news/world/asia/articles/2010/02/24/karzai_government_rewrites_afghan_election_law/ (accessed July 6, 2010).

94. Human Rights Watch, "The 'ten-dollar Talib' and women's rights," 22.

Chapter 4

1. United Nations General Assembly, "A more secure world: our shared responsibility," Report of the High-level Panel on Threats, Challenges and Change, A/59/565 (New York: United Nations, December 2004), par. 148.

2. United Nations General Assembly, "In larger freedom: towards development, security, and human rights for all," Report of the Secretary-General, A/59/2005 (New York: United Nations, March 21, 2005), par. 14, 17.

3. United Nations General Assembly, "United Nations General Assembly Resolution 60/288: The United Nations Global Counter-Terrorism Strategy," A/RES/60/288 (New York: United Nations, September 20, 2006), Annex (pillar I).

4. David Wildman and Phyllis Bennis, *Ending the US War in Afghanistan: A Primer* (Northampton, MA: Olive Branch Press, 2010), 76.

5. U.S. House of Representatives Committee on Armed Services, Subcommittee on Oversight and Investigations, "Agency stovepipes versus strategic agility: lessons we need to learn from provincial reconstruction teams in Iraq and Afghanistan," 72 (April 2008), http://armedservices.house.gov/pdfs/Reports/PRT_Report.pdf (accessed October 20, 2010).

6. Stewart Patrick and Kaysie Brown, "The Pentagon and global development: making sense of the DoD's expanding role" (working paper 131, Center for Global Development, Washington, DC, November 2007), 5–6.

7. ActionAid, et al., "Quick impact, quick collapse: the dangers of militarized aid in Afghanistan" (Oxfam International, January 2010), 1–3, http://www.oxfam.org/sites/www.oxfam.org/files/quick-impact-quick-collapse-jan-2010.pdf (accessed September 8, 2010). The eight organizations contributing to this report were ActionAid, Afghanaid, CARE, Christian Aid, Concern, Norwegian Refugee Council (NRC), Oxfam, and Trócaire.

8. David Kilcullen, *The Accidental Guerrilla: Fighting Small Wars in the Midst of a Big One* (Oxford: Oxford University Press, 2009), 102.

9. U.S. Army Combined Arms Center, "Commanders' guide to money as a weapons system: tactics, techniques, and procedures," April 2009.

10. ActionAid, et al., "Quick impact, quick collapse," 1.

11. The Code of Conduct for the International Red Cross and Red Crescent Movement and NGOs in Disaster Relief (Geneva: ICRC, 1994), www.icrc.org/web/eng/siteeng0.nsf/htmlall/code-of-conduct-290296 (accessed October 7, 2010).

12. Kilcullen, *Accidental Guerrilla*, 66.

13. Mark Duffield, "Human Security: Linking Development and Security in an Age of Terror," in *New Interfaces Between Security and Development: Changing Concepts and Approaches*, ed. Stephan Klingebiel, 11–38 (Bonn, Ger.: Deutsches Institut für Entwicklungspolitik, 2006), 30–31.

14. "Towards a culture of security and accountability," The Report of the Independent Panel on Safety and Security of UN Personnel and Premises Worldwide, June 9, 2008, paras. 269, 279, 285. Available online at *UN News Centre*, http://www.un.org/News/dh/infocus/terrorism/PanelOnSafetyReport.pdf (accessed September 18, 2008).

15. ACBAR bulletin obtained December 27, 2002, quoted in Christopher Holshek and Kevin M. Cahill, ed., *The Pulse of Humanitarian Assistance* (New York: Fordham University Press, 2007), 110.

16. Kilcullen, *Accidental Guerrilla*, 91, 107–109.

17. Ibid., 96–97.

18. Marika Theros and Mary Kaldor, "Building Afghan Peace from the Ground Up," unpublished draft paper, November 15, 2010.

19. Matt Waldman, "Falling Short: Aid Effectiveness in Afghanistan," ACBAR Advocacy Series, March 28, 2008.

20. Organisation for Economic Co-operation and Development, "A development co-operation lens on terrorism prevention: key entry points for action," DAC Reference Document, 2003, 11. Available online at the OECD, http://www.oecd.org/dataoecd/17/4/16085708.pdf (accessed August 13, 2008).

21. Coopération Internationale pour le Développement et la Solidarité, "CIDSE study on security and development," CIDSE Reflection Paper, January 2006, 19. Available online at CIDSE, http://www.cidse.org/docs/200601261245255104.pdf (accessed October 10, 2008).

22. Clive Robinson, "Whose Security? Integration and Integrity in EU Policies for Security and Development," in *New Interfaces Between Security and Development: Changing Concepts and Approaches*, ed. Stephan Klingebiel, 69–92 (Bonn, Ger.: Deutsches Institut für Entwicklungspolitik, 2006), 75, 81.

23. ActionAid, et al., "Quick impact, quick collapse," 3–4.

Chapter 5

1. Gilles Dorronsoro, "Focus and Exit: An Alternative Strategy for the Afghan War" (position paper, Carnegie Endowment for International Peace, January 2009, Washington, DC), 2.

2. Barnett R. Rubin and Ahmed Rashid, "From great game to grand bargain: ending chaos in Afghanistan and Pakistan," *Foreign Affairs* 87, no. 6 (November/December 2008): 32.

3. "Support for U.S. efforts plummets amid Afghanistan's ongoing strife," *Afghanistan: Where Things Stand* (ABC News/BBC/ARD poll, February 9, 2009), 12. Available at *ABC News*, http://abcnews.go.com/images/PollingUnit/1083a1Afghanistan2009.pdf (accessed July 5, 2009).

4. Antonio Giustozzi, *Koran, Kalashnikov, and Laptop: The Neo-Taliban Insurgency in Afghanistan* (New York: Columbia University Press, 2008), 136.

5. Dexter Filkins, "US pullout a condition in Afghan peace talks," *New York Times,* May 20, 2009.

6. Thom Shanker, David E. Sanger, and Eric Schmitt, "U.S. aids Taliban to attend talks on making peace," *New York Times,* October 14, 2010, A1.

7. Jean MacKenzie, "Former Taliban officials offer insight on how talks can progress," *The Huffington Post,* March 24, 2009, http://www .huffingtonpost.com/2009/03/24/former-taliban-officials_n_178530.html (accessed September 30, 2009).

8. Thomas Ruttig, *How Tribal Are the Taleban?: Afghanistan's Largest Insurgent Movement Between Its Tribal Roots and Islamist Ideology* (Afghanistan Analysts Network), AAN Thematic Report 04/2010, 18.

9. Rubin and Rashid, "From great game to grand bargain," 39.

10. Giustozzi, *Koran, Kalashnikov, and Laptop,* 134, 206–209.

11. Michael Semple, *Reconciliation in Afghanistan* (Washington, DC: United States Institute of Peace Press, 2009), 5, 32.

12. David Kilcullen, *The Accidental Guerrilla: Fighting Small Wars in the Midst of a Big One* (Oxford: Oxford University Press, 2009), 49.

13. Ruttig, *How Tribal Are the Taleban?,* 3.

14. Selig S. Harrison, "How to leave Afghanistan without losing," *Foreign Policy* online, August 24, 2010, http://www.foreignpolicy.com/ articles/2010/08/24/how_to_leave_afghanistan_without_losing (accessed August 25, 2010).

15. Stephen Biddle, Fotina Christia, and J. Alexander Thier, "Defining success in Afghanistan: what can the United States accept?" *Foreign Affairs* 89, no. 4 (July/August 2010), 51.

16. Ibid., 59.

17. Harrison, "How to leave Afghanistan without losing."

18. *A New Way Forward: Rethinking U.S. Strategy in Afghanistan,* Report of the Afghanistan Study Group, August 16, 2010, http://www .afghanistanstudygroup.com/.

19. Harrison, "How to leave Afghanistan without losing."

20. Sumit Ganguly and Nicholas Howenstein, "India-Pakistan rivalry in Afghanistan," *Journal of International Affairs* 63, no. 1 (Fall/Winter 2009): 128.

21. Vishal Chandra, "The Afghan elections and the Bonn process: assessing India's options," *Strategic Analysis* 29, no. 4 (2005): 727.

22. Ganguly and Howenstein, "India-Pakistan rivalry in Afghanistan," 129, 132.

23. International Crisis Group, "Pakistan: the militant jihadi challenge," Asia Report No 164 (Brussels: International Crisis Group, March 2009), ii, http://www.crisisgroup.org/~/media/Files/asia/south-asia/pakistan/164_pakistan___the_militant_jihadi_challenge.ashx (accessed August 22, 2010).

24. See Anwar Iqbal, "Hillary urges rich Pakistanis to pay more taxes," *Dawn*, February 26, 2010, http://www.dawn.com/wps/wcm/connect/dawn-content-library/dawn/the-newspaper/front-page/19-hillary-urges-rich-pakistanis-to-pay-more-tax-for-selfreliance-620-hh-03federal budget.

25. Eric Schmitt and David E. Sanger, "Pakistani troops linked to abuses will lose U.S. aid," *New York Times*, October 22, 2010, A12.

26. James Dobbins, "How to talk to Iran," *Washington Post*, July 22, 2007, http://www.washingtonpost.com/wp-dyn/content/article/2007/07/20/AR2007072002056.html (accessed October 7, 2010).

27. Barbara Slavin, "Iran helped overthrow the Taliban, candidate says," *USA Today*, June 9, 2005, http://www.usatoday.com/news/world/2005-06-09-iran-taliban_x.htm (accessed October 8, 2010).

28. Giustozzi, *Koran, Kalashnikov, and Laptop*, 28–29.

29. David Wildman and Phyllis Bennis, *Ending the US War in Afghanistan: A Primer* (Northampton, MA: Olive Branch Press, 2010), 169.

Index

About the Author

David Cortright is the Director of Policy Studies at the Kroc Institute for International Peace Studies at the University of Notre Dame and Chair of the Board of the Fourth Freedom Forum.

Cortright is the author or editor of seventeen books, including most recently *Towards Nuclear Zero*, with Raimo Väyrynen (Routledge, International Institute for Strategic Studies, 2010), Adelphi 410. Other recent works include the second edition of *Gandhi and Beyond: Nonviolence for a New Political Age* (Paradigm, 2009), *Peace: A History of Movements and Ideas* (Cambridge University Press, 2008), and *Uniting Against Terror: Cooperative Nonmilitary Responses to the Global Terrorist Threat* (MIT Press, 2007), coedited with George A. Lopez. Over the past decade Cortright and Lopez have written or coedited a series of major works on multilateral sanctions, including *Smart Sanctions, Sanctions and the Search for Security,* and *The Sanctions Decade.* Cortright is also editor of *The Price of Peace: Incentives and International Conflict Prevention.*

Cortright has written widely on nonviolent social change, nuclear disarmament, and the use of multilateral sanctions and incentives as tools of international peacemaking. He has provided research services to the foreign ministries of Canada, Sweden, Finland, Switzerland, Japan, Germany, Denmark, and The Netherlands and has served as consultant or adviser to agencies of the United Nations.

Cortright has a long history of public advocacy for disarmament and the prevention of war. As an active-duty soldier during the Vietnam War he spoke against that conflict. From 1978 to 1988 Cortright was executive director of SANE, the largest disarmament organization in the United States. In November 2002 he helped to create Win Without War, a coalition of national organizations opposing the invasion and occupation of Iraq.